GLIMMER OF HOPE

This book is dedicated to:

My grandmother Chaya Aidel Düm who was
adored by all her children
and whose strength, generosity and love
inspired my mother to be who she is today.

My mother who is today and will always be
my inspiration.

My father whose determination and devotion
gave me strength and purpose.

© Anita Peleg 2014

First published in 2014 by
Anita Peleg
34 Windmill Street
London W1T 2JR
www.naomiblake.co.uk

On the occasion of the exhibition
NAOMI BLAKE: A RETROSPECTIVE
At the Curwen and New Academy Gallery
2-26 April 2016

ISBN: 978-0-9928643-1-6

Written by: Anita Peleg
Edited by: Gerald Jacobs
Proof read by: Angela Kiverstein
Designed by: Secondary Modern, London
Printed and bound by: CPI
Cover photos:
Glimmer of Hope: front cover by John Ross
Naomi with *Unbound*: back cover by Rod Shone
Shalom II: inside front cover by The Ammerdown Centre
Man Against the Odds: inside back cover by Rod Shone
Additional photo credits:
Beth Shalom Holocaust Education Centre
Bristol Post
London News Service
Map by: Free Vector Maps

GLIMMER OF HOPE

THE STORY OF NAOMI BLAKE

Written by:
ANITA PELEG

ACKNOWLEDGEMENTS

Many important people in my life have inspired me to write this book.

First and foremost my mother who is and will forever be my greatest inspiration. Her story is one of strength, courage and of the human spirit and I thank her for sharing it with me so intimately and entrusting me with the responsibility to write it. While my father only features toward the end of the book, his story of growing up in Berlin in the '30s, fighting the Fascists in the streets and his work as a Jewish socialist prior to 1939 gave me a pride and determination to express myself freely as a Jew. Without these characteristics of both my mother and my father I would not have been able to undertake this task.

Many of my parents' friends survived or escaped the camps and their contribution to our world was hugely significant. We are all in their debt for ensuring the survival of democracy and for rebuilding society after the events of the two world wars.

In particular, I must thank my mother's friends Chaya, Chana, Shoshi, Rivka, Moishe and Batsheva and my mother's sister Malchi, who all agreed to be interviewed for this book. Their testimonies were moving and extremely helpful in supporting my mother's story. Sadly Shoshi, Batsheva and Malchi are no longer with us, but I will always remember them.

In 1995 I first visited Beth Shalom Holocaust Education Centre, a remarkable place established by the Smith Family in the Nottinghamshire Countryside. Their vision to create a place of memory and education for the Holocaust and their tireless work to help survivors of genocide express their stories encouraged me to do the same for my mother. Eddie, Marina, Stephen and James, I thank you.

I started interviewing my mother and her friends for this book more than ten years ago. For much of that time I had little confidence or courage that I could do justice to such a story. It took me eight years to show my writing to anyone but I finally showed it to two trusted friends, Hugh and Katya and then to my husband Gidi who all gave me constructive and encouraging comments. Finally last year I decided to get advice from Gerald Jacobs, writer and literary editor of the Jewish Chronicle. He transformed my poor writing into a document that I am now proud of. Gerald, I thank you for helping me make this project happen. I am pretty sure I would not have succeeded without you.

I am indebted to my cousins Ada Fisher in New York, Miriam Yunger in Florida, Tommy Berkovits in Australia and Motti Schlussel in Israel, who all provided me with information and photos. Nili, Chaya's daughter and Michal, Chana's daughter also helped me with last-minute information and photos.

Thanks are also due to Angela Kiverstein who took on the job of proofing this text at very short notice and to John Morgan who magically managed to produce a map of my mother's journey. Simon Josebury of Secondary Modern did a great job with the book design, also in a very short time, immediately after completing a separate book about my mother's sculpture. Simon, thank you again for your patience and skill.

Finally, I would like to thank my husband Gidi and my son Ben, for always supporting and encouraging me. Ben was present at many of the early interview sessions with his grandmother. His interest in her story is the essence of what this book is all about.

AUTHOR'S NOTE

SOURCES: This story is based on several weeks of interviews with my mother, her sister and her friends. The information is reported from their recollection of events and supported by the following factual histories:

Berger, A., (2009) *Munkács: A Jewish World that Was*, Department of Hebrew, Biblical and Jewish Studies, The University of Sydney

Dayan, M. Gen., (1976) *Dayan Story of my Life*, Littlehampton Book Services Ltd.

Gilbert, M., (2008) *Israel: A History*, Black Swan

Jelinek, Y.A., (2007) *The Carpathian Diaspora, The Jews of Subcarpathian Rus' and Mukachevo 1848-1948*, Columbia University Press

Laquer, W., (2003) *A History of Zionism*, Tauris Parke Paperbacks

and records held by the following organisations:

Yad Vashem, Jerusalem, Israel

State of Israel Ministry of Defence, IDF & Defence Establishment Archives.

SPELLING OF NAMES AND PLACE NAMES: In referring to members of my mother's family I have used their familiar names and not their given names (for example, my mother's sister Malka was known to everyone as Malchi). In my mother's case, her given name was Zisel and she was known by everyone as Zisi. She later went through a phase of being known as Metouka by her close friends and on arrival in Palestine she changed her name to Naomi.

My mother's home town has changed hands many times. Before 1918 it was part of the Austro-Hungarian Empire; for most of the time that my mother lived there, from 1920-1938, it was ruled by Czechoslovakia; from 1939-44 it was annexed by the Hungarians and in 1944 the German army took over. In 1945 the area became part of the USSR, and today it is the Western part of the Ukraine. Under each ruler the name of the town was spelt differently.

I have spelt the name of my mother's home town *Mukačevo*, as it was spelt by the Czech regime. The majority of Jews fondly refer to the town as Munkács (the Hungarian name) or Munkatch (the German name). However, my mother's most positive memories of her childhood are from the time of the progressive Czech rule, and so together we decided to use the Czech name. Today the town is in the Ukraine and is known as Mukacheve.

The Brannau concentration camp was located near the town of Bydgoszcz in northern Poland. This is not to be confused with Braunau, Adolf Hitler's birthplace, in Austria.

NAOMI'S JOURNEY FROM 1944-1953

The map is drawn according to current day borders

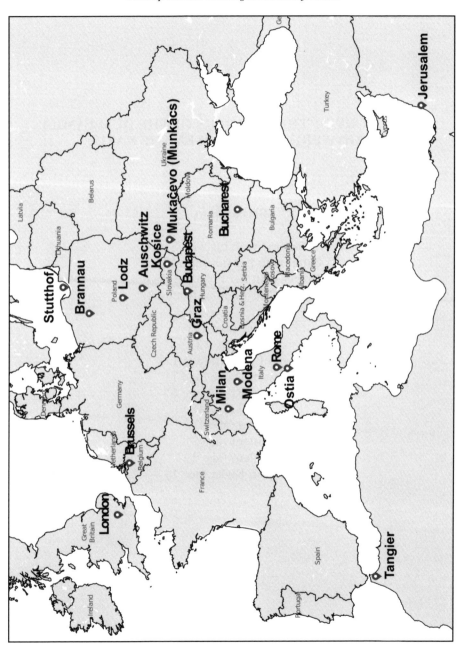

IN MEMORY OF THE MEMBERS OF THE DÜM FAMILY
WHO WERE MURDERED BY THE NAZIS:

Elazar Düm

Shloime with his wife Sara
Gittel with her husband Shoni
Esther with her husband Yossi
Mayer (husband of Ruchtu)

Asher (age 13)
Judit (age 12)
Fishel Ephraim (age 11)
Miryam Rivka (age 7)
Miryam Rivka (age 6)
Berel (age 4)
Hava (age 3)
Shulem (age 2)
Shulem (age 1)
Miryam Rivka (age 1)

THE DÜM FAMILY

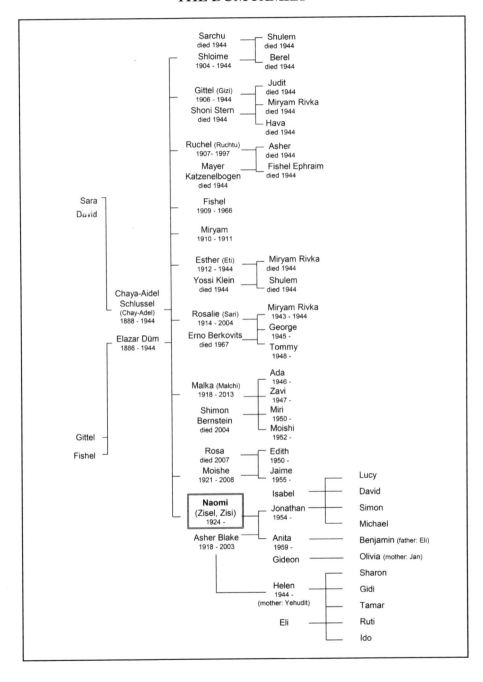

CONTENTS

INTRODUCTION

My day in Auschwitz

INTRODUCTION

My day in Auschwitz

October 2001. An unremarkable, cool and rainy morning at Luton airport. I was just one among a crowd of tired passengers, robbed of sleep in order to catch an early flight. I searched the faces surrounding me, wondering who was simply taking a tourist-trip to Krakow and who, like me, was going to Auschwitz. The flight itself was smooth enough, the only unusual incident being the hygiene check at Krakow airport. We all had to wash our hands before entering the country. An irony; some of us were here to walk on soil so stained that no amount of washing could ever cleanse it.

Aboard the coach, I looked for something odd or ugly in the countryside that I could dislike but there was nothing. The land was flat and barren-looking with patches of green and small, grey houses along the route. It all seemed almost lifeless and void of character. I focused instead on our Polish guide. As he talked, his message became very clear: "Hitler persecuted us, too; Germany destroyed our heritage and our dignity as well." The rich, enlightened, highly cultured society that once was Poland seemed to have disappeared. It certainly did not appear before me as we drove through the countryside.

Aware though I was of approaching the world's most notorious site of evil, inhuman behaviour, much of what I saw in Auschwitz surprised and shocked me. On arriving at Auschwitz One, now a museum, I expected to find a grim, muddy and bleak expanse. Instead, with the sun shining on neat paths alongside grass and trees, I was shocked at how pleasant the place looked from the outside. Perhaps this first impression made the image of what I saw inside so much more memorable. At first, it was just a museum with pictures and letters but that soon changed. I still today catch my breath when I remember the room in which, behind a glass front, approximately eight-foot-deep mounds of human hair were visible.

Behind another, smaller, viewing glass were rugs and blankets made from hair. Then came the collections of personal items amassed by the Nazis from their victims; suitcases with names, places of origin and dates of birth; thousands of pairs of round, wire-framed spectacles; piles of shoes; hairbrushes; toothbrushes; shaving brushes.

The silence that permeated the rooms housing these exhibits was broken only by gasps and stifled tears. I stood, mesmerised, for many minutes in front of the suitcases, looking for a name I recognised. After that, I could not bear to look at the display of children's shoes and sought the sunshine and fresh air. Outside, the guide resumed his explanations but I remember little of them.

In a short time, we were back on the coach and on our way to Auschwitz Two – Birkenau. This was the death camp for the largest number of Jews, in particular the Jews of Hungary. Leading our group was Rabbi Jonathan Wittenberg who, as we approached Aushwitz-Birkenau, told us that this camp had been left largely as it was at liberation in 1945 and had not been converted into a museum.

Standing at the all too hideously familiar entrance to Birkenau shattered my secret hope that it would feel different – smaller somehow, tamed – from the stark images in the books and newspapers showing the train tracks that led to extermination for so many. But the haunting image imprinted in my mind was not to be shifted. The reality was worse than I had expected, and feared.

We climbed the main watchtower from where we could see the vastness of the camp with its rows upon rows of barracks. After a short description by the guide, we were all impatient to move on and explore the place by ourselves. Rabbi Jonathan led us on to the train tracks and sat down there. We all followed suit. Lawyers, doctors, businessmen, mothers, fathers and teenagers all sat in the dirt and listened to readings from Eli Wiesel and Primo Levi. Then we stood up and started walking. It felt important to me to walk on every plank of the track. Somewhere alongside these tracks my mother had walked and stood bewildered and ignorant of what was going to happen. In my mind's eye I could visualise smoke rising from the place where the gas chambers and crematoria had once stood. I looked around at the barbed-wire fences and imagined people standing there watching me with big eyes staring from emaciated faces.

We continued walking until we came to the ruined remains of gas chambers and crematoria, bombed by the Nazis in an attempt to destroy the evidence. As I stood thinking of what had happened on that spot, I was overcome by a wave of nausea and frustration.

I was one of the first to arrive at the small memorial alongside the destroyed area. The silence felt appropriately reverent. Then, as the others appeared, came the sound of prayer and of weeping, while we remembered the victims and lit candles. As we walked back along the paths, I turned off into one of the barracks, a long, wooden building with a large, wooden door. Inside was a stone floor, a small room, bare and cold, possibly where the prisoners had washed, and, straight ahead of me, the bunks. Images of those who had occupied them and died or were tortured here came to me irresistibly. And, among those images, I found myself searching for my mother's face.

I stayed for some time alone in this barrack. When I came out, my brother told me that he had located my mother's barrack. She had told us she was housed in Block C10. But that was in the men's camp. When my brother asked the guide, he was told that C10 was indeed in the men's section but it was where Hungarian Jewish women were brought in 1944.

With only minutes left before the coach departed, we both ran to the other side of the camp where C10 was situated. Desperately, we ran from barrack to barrack until we found one that seemed to be the place in which our mother had been incarcerated. Again, those eyes stared at me from the bunks; again, I looked for my mother. My brother took photographs and then we had to run once more, fearful of missing the coach.

On the hour-and-a-half journey to Krakow, the coach remained silent. And then, as we came to the city, we experienced a moment of almost incongruous beauty as the dark, grey landscape gave way to Krakow's riverside, the grand buildings and the castle. This was the Poland that might have been.

We spent the final hour in the synagogue in the restored Jewish quarter of Krakow, where I felt a sudden, strong desire to return to Auschwitz-Birkenau. I wanted more time to explore and reflect. I wanted to see if life could be reaffirmed in the surroundings of that vast and desolate burial ground.

ZISI'S STORY

1

There was a sense of post-First World War optimism

Zisel Düm, known as Zisi, the youngest of the ten children of Elazar Düm and Chay-Adel Schlussel, was born on March 11,1924, in Mukačevo – formerly known as Munkács – in the mountains of the Subcarpathian Rus' region. This was a town that was home to a diverse population including Hungarians, Ukrainians, Russians, Ruthenians, Czechs and Germans.

It was also a town that was undergoing profound changes. In 1920, after the Treaty of Trianon, which divided up the old Austro-Hungarian empire, Munkács had officially become part of Czechoslovakia and renamed Mukačevo. Its citizens looked forward to a new, democratic freedom following the upheavals of the preceding years of war and territorial disputes between Russians, Hungarians, Austrians and Czechs.

At that time, the 13,000-strong Jewish community represented almost half of Mukačevo's total population. After the Jews had been granted religious and civic freedom by the Czech ruling government in 1918, Jewish life flourished. Some families, including Zisi's, were relatively wealthy; others were extremely poor. But there was a strong community spirit and its wealthier members gave generously to help those who were struggling with poverty. For the most part, the Jews were hardworking and supported each other. There was a sense of post-First World War optimism throughout the Jewish community and beyond.

After giving birth to Zisi, Chay-Adel Düm, who was diabetic, became very weak and was unable to breastfeed. Zisi was looked after and fed by a Russian woman who was breastfeeding her own child but had plenty of milk for two.

Zisi's childhood memories are of openness, freedom – and horse-drawn carriages! In those days, only the occasional motorised vehicle made its way along the sandy streets of the residential areas of Mukačevo, upon which there were no pavements. Children as young as three or four happily played unsupervised on those same streets. Even the youngest could just drop in on friends and relatives at any time without needing an invitation. From the moment the cry of the cockerel was heard at sunrise, there was a constantly bustling atmosphere, with neighbours gossiping outside their houses amid the sounds of cattle being taken to graze and horses bringing produce to market. Of course, it couldn't last and, before long, the motor car would gain ascendancy and things would change forever.

The street where Zisi lived was called Bereksaz. The Düm family home was accessed through heavy, wooden doors opening on to a large courtyard. To the right of the entrance to the courtyard were stone steps leading up to a terrace. Here, when she was not at work, Zisi's mother would sit and watch over the children playing.

The front door to the apartment opened into the kitchen. Before Zisi was born, part of the kitchen had been sectioned off to serve as a bedroom, firstly for Zisi's sister Malchi and later for a maid. The kitchen was the engine-room of the household. This was especially the case on Friday nights, prior to the Sabbath, and on festivals, when the maid and Zisi's sisters would all congregate there to help Chay-Adel prepare food.

The kitchen led into an enormous L-shaped space that served as dining- and living-room. On its walls – which Chay-Adel would often redecorate – hung photographs of distinguished rabbis and talmudic scholars along with a tapestry depicting the biblical patriarchs Abraham and Isaac. In one corner was a sofa-bed; in another, a three-piece suite and coffee table. There were bookshelves, too, filled with large volumes written in Hebrew. Zisi's father Elazar would study one or more of these in the morning and evening, before and after work. Zisi and her sisters would study from time to time at a small table that was also placed in this room. But its centrepiece was a capacious table at which the family ate, talked and prayed together. This main, all-purpose room also had six small windows, with wooden shutters that were always closed at night or when the family was away from home.

The rooms – including the three bedrooms – were connected by glass doors, with net curtains to maintain privacy. The bedrooms were occupied, respectively, by Zisi's parents; her two eldest sisters, Eti and Gizi, and the four youngest – Moishe, the household's only boy at that time, Sari, Malchi and Zisi herself. A range of guests stayed frequently and so this arrangement was flexible, often involving Zisi having to sleep in the same bed as Malchi or Sari.

The Düm family owned each of the properties that made up the Bereksaz terrace. Once the oldest siblings, Shloime, Fishel, Ruchtu and Gizi had grown up and left home, Elazar and Chay-Adel converted their own apartment by dividing part of it into a separate, three-room-plus-kitchen apartment, which they let out, just as they had let the three other properties that made up the rest of the building alongside the courtyard.

The courtyard was a miniature world of its own. Indoor running water was a rarity at that time and, in the courtyard where the Düm family lived, there was one pump and three toilets (which were emptied once a month by the town sanitary services). Zisi would often help the maid at the pump to collect the water in buckets and carry it inside for washing, cooking and drinking.

The members of the Düm household were always busy. Zisi's sisters helped the maid with daily chores and cooking, ensuring that there was plenty of food for their numerous visitors, who were always made welcome. Chay-Adel also made sure that additional food was prepared for less-fortunate neighbours and friends who had little to eat. The Düm children were encouraged to deliver these gifts of food.

Then there was the family business to run. Zisi's older sisters were often absent for several hours helping their mother and father run the small textile store in the centre of town. While Zisi's mother was working in the shop, Zisi was cared for at home by her older sister Eti and Helen, the live-in maid. Helen took her everywhere, perched on her large hip, sometimes accompanied by her boyfriend. In this way, Zisi was taken to places where the orthodox Düm family never ventured. Visits to the local fair and the circus remain among the most vivid of her memories.

2

On one occasion, the bathing ritual was followed by
a bareback ride through the centre of town

Zisi's grandfather, Rav David Schlussel, was an eminent figure in Mukačevo. He was the chief justice of the Mukačevo rabbinical courts and a prominent follower of the Munkatcher Rebbe. Zisi and Malchi loved to walk to their grandfather's house, where there was always a warm welcome. Zisi would rush to kiss his hand and sit close to him as she enjoyed the delicious bread or cake made by her grandmother. There she would also meet her numerous cousins (Rav David had nine children and therefore many grandchildren) and particularly enjoyed the company of Zishka, Kiwi and Libshe, to name but a few. David Schlussel had a long, white beard, through which his soft, round face would break into a tender smile as he embarked on stories of the family's wise and just ancestors and of learned scholars. He was known to be kind-hearted and fair-minded and many people came to seek his guidance and advice. Zisi loved to sit nearby and listen to Rav David's deliberations on such occasions. She was quite often present when people would come to ask her grandfather to check the suitability of chickens for consumption.

In those days, chickens were bought live from the market or from individual tradesmen and fed by the owner until they were considered ready to be killed. The family, usually in the shape of the owner's wife, would then take the chicken to the shochet – the butcher – who would kill the chicken according to Jewish religious law. It was the duty of the family to see that the chicken was checked for signs of disease which would render it unkosher and therefore not fit for consumption. David Schlussel was widely trusted and many women sought his approval before despatching the chicken to the pot.

Zisi eavesdropped on many a conversation between Grandfather David and one of the women who would bring their chickens to him. Rav Schlussel would gently question the woman about her financial circumstances and ask how and if her husband was employed. When the family was in financial difficulty, Rav Schlussel would be inclined to turn a blind eye over any doubt about the chicken's condition and allow the family to have it slaughtered for their table.

Zisi and her brother and sister, Moishe and Malchi, loved to play in the courtyard – often under the watchful eye of their mother, Chay-Adel – with Baruche, Chagite and Chayeta, the children of the families renting their property. The courtyards were not their only playground. They frequently played in the streets, where Zisi had three very close friends: Mogda, Yenti and Yitte.

Zisi's schooldays were mostly very happy. She was popular both with the teachers and with her fellow pupils. Once, she experienced a prolonged absence from school following a near-fatal infection from a nail that had become lodged in her foot and, on her return, she was given an emotional welcome back by her teacher.

Before and after school she loved to climb the fruit trees opposite her house, picking and eating dates and pears with her friends Mogda, Yenti and Yitte. She also enjoyed walking to school, at first with her sister Eti and later with her street-friends.

In those early Mukačevo mornings, as Zisi looked out of her window at the break of dawn, she could see her father and other Chasidic men, in their distinctive wide-brimmed black hats and long side-locks, black trousers and jackets, hurrying to synagogue. Each man carried his white prayer-shawl – the *talit* – wrapped up under one arm. Jewish tradesmen, workers, clerks and teachers were also in evidence, their heads covered by brown hats or caps. Hanging from all the men's pale shirts and dark coats were the fringed garments – *tzitzit* – that they wore as reminders of the need for holiness and prayer. A favourite sight would be that of Yitte's father, the baker, loading up his horse and cart with freshly baked bread to sell in the market.

By the time Zisi was up and dressed, the streets would be full of people– children walking to school, their mothers chatting, men on their way to study or to work and tradesmen delivering and selling their merchandise. Sometimes, the noise of arguments between neighbours could be heard across the courtyard. Screams and shrieks would also issue from the open windows of Zisi's own home as her sisters argued over stockings and other items of clothing while Chay-Adel tried to calm her daughters.

With no treatment for her diabetes available locally, Chay-Adel continued to struggle with poor health. Accordingly, she would often spend a few summer weeks at a spa in Karlsbad. While Chay-Adel was away, Zisi, Moishe and Malchi were sent to stay with a Jewish family, who took in paying guests, on a farm in the beautiful mountain surroundings of Skotarsko.

As a tiny child of six or so, Zisi ate very little and so Chay-Adel would ask the farmer's wife to be sure to give her youngest daughter lots of cream with her food.

At the Skotarsko farm, Zisi would be woken every morning at 4am, the start of the farm's working day, with a hot cup of foaming milk straight from the cow. With plenty of children to play with who were staying at other farms in the area, these summer holidays were idyllic. They were also a rare privilege. Not only could most of the Düms' neighbours, Jewish and non-Jewish, not afford a holiday, many could not even imagine what a holiday was like. Among these were the families of Zisi's friends from the street and so she was always especially eager to see them on her return. She would also be excited to be back home with her dearest sister Eti and her mother.

Mukačevo was an important centre of Chasidic Judaism, with different sects headed by different rabbis, known as Rebbes. Zisi's friend Modga was from an extremely poor family who followed the traditions of the Belzer Rebbe while her friend Yenti's family were adherents of the Munkatcher Rebbe.

The Munkatcher and Belzer Rebbes were often at odds. They and their followers were even, at times, sworn enemies. Families were forbidden to talk to each other. The disputes usually centred on some minute difference of interpretation of something in the Talmud but became so heated that meetings would be disrupted and physical fights break out. Not everybody took these matters so seriously, however. The children, in particular, showed a healthy disregard for such feuding. Zisi's street-friends Mogda and Yenti were both forbidden to talk to each other but, outside on the streets, they paid no attention to their parents' strictures and they were inseparable.

It was through Yitte that Zisi's free-spirited nature blossomed. Yitte's father, Nachum the baker, owned two horses, and Zisi doted on them. At the age of six or seven, she would go with Yitte to wash the horses in the nearby river. The horses responded warmly to Zisi and would affectionately rub their noses against her. She loved to go into the river with them to bathe. On one occasion, this bathing ritual was followed by a bareback ride through the centre of town to Yitte's house. Heedless of her status as the daughter of a respected shop-owner and religious scholar and the granddaughter of the head of the rabbinical court of Mukačevo, Zisi shocked onlookers.

Her bareback ride became something of a family legend. As she rode past her father's shop, he had to blink twice to make sure that he was really seeing his youngest daughter exhibiting herself in this way. That night, he expressed his disapproval by maintaining a cool silence. Thereafter, although their exploits with the horses in the river increased, Zisi and Yitte either chose quiet side-streets along which to ride the horses or simply walked them home. Even so, for months afterwards, Elazar often asked Zisi with stern affection about "Nachum's *pferd*" (Nachum's horse).

As the youngest in the family, Zisi was fortunate in that, while her unorthodox behaviour could certainly upset her parents, her path had to some extent been cleared by her elder brothers and sisters. By the time her mother and father had to deal with her spirited and independent personality, they were well seasoned in the wiles and ways of lively children and so generally took a more tolerant, liberal approach to Zisi.

In any case, this was the age of rebellion; many children of orthodox religious families were joining different Zionist and Socialist groups that defied the beliefs of their parents. Others remained religious but the young men shaved their beards and the young women took on a more "modern" look, in line with the latest fashion trends, while still upholding the traditions of their faith. A minority had given up religion altogether and were on their way towards assimilation into Czech society. As for Zisi, while she was still a child, her indiscretions were considered only minor. In time, however, it would become apparent that they had been the first stirrings of an independent mind that would later embrace left-wing Zionist ideology.

Zisi mixed easily with both Jewish and non-Jewish children. Two of the latter with whom she had particularly close friendships were Trudi and Kurt. One Jewish friendship that was frowned upon was with a boy called Eliezer, the son of a Zionist family, who sent him to the Hebrew Gymnasium. This was a school of which Zisi's father deeply disapproved.

While lunch was the main meal of the day in the Düm household, the evening meal was the only time when the whole family would come together. The young Zisi and her brothers and sisters would instinctively know when it was time to go home for supper and at that point would leave the company of their friends and relatives. As they walked, they would encounter the cows also making their way home through the streets, to the accompaniment of the herdsman's gong and the cowbells around the animals' necks. Having been taken to the mountains to graze, they were being brought back before sunset, in time, just like the children, to find their own way to their respective homes.

3

The young Jews spoke Czech among themselves, while their parents persisted with Hungarian

The area of the Carpathian Mountains in which Mukačevo was situated was primarily agrarian with a high degree of poverty. Along with the gradual emergence of the motor car, electricity did not become widespread until the 1930s. In the midst of this, Mukačevo stood out as a vibrant centre of learning and commerce and consequently attracted people from the surrounding area. Its inhabitants spoke a number of languages. During the time of Austro-Hungarian rule, there were several different schools, Russian, Hungarian or German, and the national language was Hungarian. Jewish families were brought up additionally speaking Yiddish and reading Hebrew.

In the period between the two world wars, Mukačevo continued to thrive as a centre of religious Judaism. It boasted several *Chasidic yeshivas* – religious colleges for the study of Judaism – as well as Jewish printing houses and Jewish schools. But the secular and Zionist communities, with which Zisi came to align herself, also grew in significance during those years. The prestigious Hebrew Gymnasium – which Zisi's friend Eliezer attended – was established in 1925 and was the first high-school in Czechoslovakia to teach modern Hebrew and the principles of Zionism.

For the two decades of Czech rule, from 1918-1938, a more uniform education system was imposed under which students attended Czech schools and were taught the Czech national language. Thus, a cultural rift rapidly developed between the younger and older generations. Zisi's parents and friends, like their non-Jewish counterparts, were fervently patriotic Hungarians. They continued to speak Hungarian in the streets – still referring to their home town as Munkács – and longed for the days of Hungarian rule. The young, however, under the compulsory Czech education, not only spoke Czech in school but became familiar with the democratic principles and philosophy of the Czech government. This was in marked contrast to the old Austro-Hungarian discipline to which their parents' generation was subjected. Under the Czech president, Tomas Masaryk, Jews were granted official minority status and given both religious freedom and equal status. Jewish and even openly Zionist parties were allowed by the regime.

In this new climate, young Jews and non-Jews grew fiercely proud of their Czech culture of democracy and religious freedom. At the same time, they tended to regard the Hungarian language and traditions as symbols of the old autocracies. This all made for a complex linguistic mixture in the home of the Düms and other Jewish families. Like their non-Jewish counterparts, the young Jews spoke Czech among themselves, while their parents persisted with Hungarian. In addition, among the Jews, Yiddish was spoken at home and their religious lessons were in biblical Hebrew and, as the Zionist movement grew, many studied modern Hebrew as well.

Russian and German were also taught in schools and Zisi and her sisters were taught German at home by a private tutor. Perforce, the Düm children acquired a facility for languages. They learnt Czech and Hungarian using the Latin alphabet; Hebrew using the Hebrew alphabet; Russian, the Russian alphabet and German, the Gothic.

Prior to the Czech occupation, families chose between Russian, Hungarian or German schools. Zisi's older sisters went to Russian school but, by the time Zisi was born, all children were required to go to Czech school. The Czech teachers tended to be very idealistic, believing themselves to be on a mission to educate the "primitive" people of Carpathia in the ways of Czech language and culture.

Although Zisi very much enjoyed her early school years, as she got older she became disenchanted. She found the flexibility of home, where she received extra lessons from private tutors brought to the house by her mother, much more appealing than the regimented approach of school. It also suited her growing sense of independence inspired by her membership of the Zionist Socialist Youth Movement, Hashomer Hatzair (The Young Guard), in her teenage years.

Formal schooling for Jewish girls ended at the age of 15 but Zisi's mother defied this convention and continued to encourage her daughters to learn, particularly German and music. German was considered the language of culture and enlightenment. Zisi had done a little German at school but it was her mother's insistence on bringing in a private tutor for her older sisters, while the boys stayed on at school, that also reinforced and expanded Zisi's knowledge.

Relations between Mukačevo's Jews and non-Jews were good. Most of the houses on Zisi's street were occupied by Jewish families but it was not an exclusively Jewish area. And the neighbours were invariably polite when they encountered one another on the local street or in the busy town centre, with its one central main street, market square, town hall and clock tower, ten minutes' walk away.

This was where the Düm family textile shop and Zisi's sister Gizi's fur shop were situated, among the many other fabric merchants, food shops and others selling household goods. Here, too, people would gather on national holidays and the young girls would admire the Czech soldiers on parade.

The textile shop was close to the market, where things got going very early with farmers and traders arriving with their produce. The business benefited from passers-by dropping into the shops on their way to or from the market. The work was tiring and, as the evenings wore on, the girls would eagerly look across the road and count the minutes on the town-hall clock before they could close up at 7pm and make their way home.

The shop had been established by Zisi's mother and grandmother, soon after Chay-Adel and Elazar were married. Later, when Elazar became involved, he propelled the business towards greater success. Zisi loved to go to the shop and soak up the atmosphere. She particularly enjoyed watching her sisters Sari and Eti unravelling rolls of beautifully coloured fabrics to show the customers, discussing colour schemes and dresses, cutting the fabric with special long scissors and organising the window displays. Of all her sisters, Sari had the greatest sales talent and would wrap the fabrics around herself in order to show the customer how they might look on her. Sari's beauty, wit and eye for colour were real assets for the business. Eti was more down-to-earth; she would often scold Sari for immodesty in the manner in which she draped herself in the various materials. But Sari paid no attention to her sister and carried on in her own high-spirited – and commercially effective – way.

Chay-Adel, meanwhile, quietly got on with managing the accounts and the purchasing. She became a respected businesswoman, known for her good relationships with suppliers and clients and, most of all, for her generous and kind disposition. This, along with the efficient salesmanship of the girls, guaranteed that the store was always full of both friends and customers.

Later, when Eti and Gizi had married and left home, Zisi and Malchi helped Sari in the shop, allowing their mother, whose health was deteriorating, to have some respite. This was especially important when their father was travelling to purchase new fabrics and supplies. Over time, Sari and the girls developed some clever strategies. Between two and five in the afternoon, when many people would stroll through the town window-shopping, the Düm girls would make sure that a lot of loosely strewn remnants were on display, creating the impression that there were many bargains to be had inside. This would lure people into the store, where of course there would be a great deal more than remnants to tempt them.

Elazar's presence in the store attracted a rather different kind of clientele. Known to many as *Lotsi Batchi* (Uncle Lotsi), he was considered to be a patient listener and a man of wisdom and integrity. Accordingly, many Jewish men and women would frequent the store when they knew he would be there, not only to buy something, but also to seek his advice on family and financial matters. Elazar's adoption of this role puzzled and amused the girls as it was one that he never managed to bring home to his family.

4

She believed that kissing might suck the goodness out of the child

Zisı's arrival as the youngest of the ten children born to Chay-Adel Schlussel and Elazar Düm, was preceded by the birth of three brothers and six sisters (one of whom, Miryam, died after just a few months of life) – spanning a period of 20 years. By the time Zisi was two years old, and able to remember, four of her siblings had grown up and moved out of the parental home. By 1943, the family, including four grandparents, had become extended to include the older children's six spouses and ten grandchildren, a total of 31 direct family members. Three years later, only eight family members remained. The rest of the family, including all of the grandchildren, had been murdered.

The marriage of Chay-Adel to Elazar was a traditional one, arranged between their two families. Zisi's and her siblings' recollections of her mother show her to have been a remarkable woman. Though in poor health for much of her married life, she was energetic, caring and generous. Early every Friday morning, for example, Zisi watched her wrap coins and banknotes inside pieces of newspaper. Chay-Adel would then tell Zisi to deliver these gift parcels to nearby families in need.

Right from the start of her marriage, Chay-Adel showed great enterprise in finding ways to support her husband – who was intent on a life of learning and prayer – and her family. She began by selling fabrics from a market stall, which proved to be the springboard for a successful textile business based on the shop in the centre of town. She had an astute business brain and a well-merited reputation for fairness and honesty. And she was certainly no stop-at-home housewife. Despite having nine living children, Chay-Adel did not spend a lot of time in the home; she spent as much time as possible at work in her textile business, which she loved. As her eldest sons and daughters grew, responsibility fell upon them for the everyday care of the younger children. This worked well; there was little resentment from the children but, rather, they all cherished the time they were at home and, indeed, loved to go to the shop.

Chay-Adel's management of the day-to-day finances of the business gave her the opportunity to use that money to elevate the lifestyle and education of her family without her husband even knowing. The children were always amused when their father would parade before them every month expressing how proud he was of owning one, solitary, tailor-made suit, thereby saving money and proving how long one suit could last. Little did he know that his wife had arranged for the tailor to make several versions of the same suit, which she kept hidden away and brought out, one at a time, when the original and each subsequent suit started to look worn. "You see," he would say, lecturing the children, "you shouldn't waste money buying new clothes all the time. Look how long this one suit has lasted me." Whenever he said this, the children would smile to themselves.

Women of Chay-Adel's generation and background generally received no formal education. But she determinedly taught herself and believed strongly that all children should be taught languages, literature and music. Chay-Adel thought that the teaching at school, especially of German, was not thorough enough and, though the boys continued at school, the girls benefited from the more expert tuition at home.

Again going against the prevailing outlook, even though Chay-Adel held deep religious convictions, she nevertheless encouraged Zisi to read the modern literature of the day – something that many orthodox Jews would have considered profane. She continued to encourage Zisi to read, even when Zisi became active in left-wing Zionist youth groups and her reading material began to include the work of Karl Marx and other left-wing writers – forbidden in their community.

Chay-Adel was dearly loved by all her children, who were always ready to listen to her, follow her instructions and to emulate her behaviour. Her strength of character, intelligence, determination and resolve lay quietly beneath a calm and serene disposition. She in turn was devoted to her children. At night, she would come to each child's bedside and caress them all, breathing softly and putting her face to her child's. But she would never kiss them. She believed that kissing might suck the goodness out of the child. At her funeral, in 1944, people from all over town came to pay tribute to this industrious, loving and generous woman.

By contrast, Zisi's father, Elazar Düm, was a serious, tough and very learned man of little warmth, particularly in his early days as a young father and husband. He was especially strict with his three sons. The elder two, Shloime and Fishel, were expected to work with him in the shop, which temporarily adopted the name "Düm Brothers". However, the two young men were unable to tolerate their father's strictness and controlling nature. They clashed frequently and so furiously that they both left Mukačevo for several years in order to gain some independence.

While not quite as severe with his daughters, for whom his expectations were not so high, Elazar did not form warm bonds with any of them – except for Zisi. He did not involve himself in chatter or small talk, nor did he take an interest in his daughters' studies. In keeping with the tradition still followed in his orthodox Jewish circles, Elazar Düm believed that education was for men alone and not for women. Thus, he had little to discuss with his young, independent-minded girls – even though all of them had a strong thirst for knowledge and were eager to discuss literature, philosophy and Jewish learning.

Instead, their father would immerse himself in his books and spend many hours studying alone in the corner of the large dining/sitting room or together with other like-minded men in the nearby *yeshiva* – religious school. Like many young men in that society, Elazar started out with aspirations to become a rabbi, following in his father's footsteps, and spent a large part of the early years of his marriage studying towards this goal. But when he saw how his young wife had managed to establish a successful business he decided to join her in managing the shop.

Chay-Adel managed the day-to-day running of the shop, while Elazar put his efforts into expanding the business and purchasing textiles to sell. This saw him travelling to Budapest and other large cities. The arrangement worked well and the business, and therefore the family, prospered. And Elazar still managed to keep up his study of Tanach and Talmud, books dedicated to discussion of the Bible and the Jewish Law, devoting many long hours to it. He would rise early in the morning and go to the synagogue to say his morning prayers. He would then spend a couple of hours studying before making his way to the town's main street to open up the shop. When he was not travelling, Elazar would spend the whole day in the shop, taking a break only to go home and have his lunch, returning soon afterwards in order to give his wife or one of his sons or daughters time to go home and eat as well.

In the evenings, Elazar would sit at the head of the large family table, often remaining silent while the children and their mother chatted about the day's events. Nevertheless, though he appeared to be indifferent to the conversation, he would from time to time interject with a comment or question. He would always try to engage his son Moishe in discussion and ask him questions about the Torah – and would then be surprised when one or other of his daughters would interrupt to join in the conversation and demonstrate her knowledge. Despite her father's stern, unappreciative responses to these forays, Zisi was sure that he was quietly proud of his daughters' knowledge and intelligence but didn't know how to show it to them.

Unable to learn from his failed relationships with his older sons, Elazar subjected Moishe to the same critical and controlling behaviour. As the only boy still living at home, Moishe was often the object of teasing or tickling by his sisters. They would take it in turns to sit next to him and jab him while his father was talking to him or when he was asked to say the blessings at the beginning or end of every meal. Poor Moishe would squeak and squirm, causing the girls to dissolve into fits of giggles. Elazar, however, was not amused. He was very impatient towards Moishe, who, by contrast, was doted on by all the girls and especially by Chay-Adel.

After dinner, Elazar would resume his studies, either by candlelight at the table in the corner of the room or at the yeshiva along with the many other men who would congregate in the mornings and evenings for discourse or study. As a result, the Düm children grew up knowing little of their father, other than as a stern patriarch, a closed individual with whom it was difficult to connect.

Elazar's relationship with Chay-Adel, Zisi's mother, was something else that caused a rift between the children and their father. All the children adored their mother, who was an extremely warm person, devoted to giving the best to her children in every way possible. This did not prevent their father from upsetting her with his stubborn, dictatorial nature and the children witnessed many unpleasant rows between their parents.

Zisi felt a great sense of anger towards her father over the way he treated her mother but never dared to intervene. On the other hand, she sensed that her father loved her mother very much and admired Chay-Adel's quiet way of dealing with his uncompromising attitude – whether over money, which he did not like to spend, the management of the shop, or the upbringing of his children.

Unexpectedly, perhaps, as Zisi grew into a quietly rebellious young woman, this did not alienate her father. In fact, his reaction was quite the opposite. After initially concealing her views, her subsequent openness about her life-style prompted her father to show some interest in what she was doing. While he did not approve of Zisi's involvement with socialism or her liberal thinking, he would often ask her what she was reading and secretly read the same books in order to see what the modern writers and thinkers were saying.

As Elazar grew older, surrounded only by his youngest daughters at home and his grandchildren, he gradually started to embrace the changing times. As a result of this slight mellowing and the events that were to follow, Zisi and her father grew very close.

5

*When he did eventually return home, it was as a young adult that
he first saw his newborn, youngest sister*

As Zisi grew older, her family appeared to go through a number of
transformations. As a small child, she was often one of only five children
around the table, the others being Malchi, Sari, Eti and Moishe. She seemed
to spend most of her time with Moishe and Malchi, who were closest in age
to her. But the dynamics of the family were constantly shifting.

Throughout her early childhood, Zisi was particularly close to Eti (whom she
used to call "Achi"), the oldest sister living at home, who in many ways was
like a mother to Zisi. While Chaya was at work, it was Eti who cared for Zisi at
home and went to see her teachers at school. Zisi adored her "Achi" above all
her sisters but, in 1934, Eti, then 21, was introduced to Yossi Klein, a young
man from Topolchani in Macedonia. They were married soon afterwards and
Eti left the family home in Mukačevo to raise a family in Topolchani.

Zisi was broken-hearted when Eti left home but in time came to look
forward eagerly to her big sister's visits back to the family, which came round
three or four times a year. It became especially exciting in later years when
Eti and Yossi would be accompanied by their children, Zisi's niece and nephew, Miryam and Shulem. On these occasions, the large table at the Bereksaz
home became filled with new life and laughter as Eti and her husband would
share their news and Miryam and Shulem would enjoy the attention of their
grandparents, aunts and uncles – and their cousins, Gizi's children.

The family was often joined at the dinner table by Gizi – Zisi's oldest
sister and second oldest sibling – while her husband was travelling. Gizi also
lived in Mukačevo where she ran the fur shop in the same street as the family
textile business. Gizi had left home to be married before Zisi was born.
During her time at home, Gizi had taken charge of Malchi, then the youngest
girl, looking after her schooling and generally acting like a second mother,
much as Eti would do later towards Zisi.

At the age of 18, Gizi was reluctantly married to a young man called Shoni Stern. As part of her dowry, Elazar provided her and her new husband with the fur shop. This guaranteed that Gizi would remain in Mukačevo and stay close to her siblings. Like all of the Düm girls, Gizi was a beautiful young woman. She had a strong personality, which helped her to manage the fur shop efficiently but led to frequent clashes with her husband, Shoni.

While Gizi looked after the shop in Mukačevo, Shoni would spend a lot of time away in search of new materials. At such times, Gizi – and her children, Judit, Miriam and Hava – would seek the company of her mother and sisters. Zisi came to adore Gizi's children and loved their frequent appearances at the Düm household. Such visits brought out the best in Zisi's father. Normally, he was silent and withdrawn but when his grandchildren were around, he would sit them on his knee and, beaming and laughing, play with them. This was truly out of character; apart from Zisi, none of his own children could recall sitting on their father's lap – or even enjoying anything other than a slightly cool and distant relationship with him.

Less frequent visitors to the Düm household, other than on the odd weekend or Jewish festival, were Shloime and his wife and children. To Zisi, Shloime, 20 years her elder, seemed more like an uncle than a brother. He, too, had left home well before Zisi was born, having fought quite a battle with his harsh father to gain some degree of independence. So bitter were the feuds between father and son that, at the age of 16, Shloime left home, and ceased working in the family business. He spent several years in Belgium, studying and working. When he did eventually return home, it was as a young adult that he first saw his newborn, youngest sister.

A smallish man with a close resemblance to his mother, as a mark of independence characteristic of the young men of his age he had shaved off his beard and cut off his *peyot* (side-locks). But he remained religiously observant and, soon after his return, agreed to a marriage arranged by his parents, with Sara, known as Sarchu, a young woman from Kosice, in Slovakia. The couple were invited by Sarchu's parents to set up home and a business in Kosice, 50 miles from Mukačevo – and Elazar, Shloime's domineering father.

In 1941, Shloime, along with the majority of young Jewish males in the area, was ordered by the Hungarian regime to go to *Munkatabor*, the Hungarian Forced Labour Battalion, to help the war effort. While prohibited from joining the army and holding a gun, these young men were forced to do heavy construction work and clear mine fields. The German-allied Hungarian regime subjected them to extreme brutality and many never returned. During this period, Zisi travelled to Kosice to help Sarchu with her children, Shulem and Berel, as Sarchu waited for news of her husband.

One day when Zisi was five, she was surprised to see a smiling, young and handsome male visitor. His name was Fishel, and he kept Chay-Adel, Eti, Sari and Gizi continually entertained. Zisi looked at Fishel, from the comfort of Eti's lap, with a mixture of caution and curiosity. After a while, Fishel turned to Zisi and announced: "I have a special gift for my little sister. Come with me." Fishel was her brother! He took Zisi by the hand and led her out into the courtyard, followed by their brothers and sisters. There in the courtyard was a little black-and-white dog that 20-year-old Fishel had brought for Zisi, his youngest sister. Overjoyed, Zisi immediately named the dog Fidi.

Fishel was the second oldest of the Düm sons. Like his brother Shloime, he rebelled from an early age against his father's controlling hand and moved away to study in Belgium when Zisi was just a baby. At 20, however, he returned to live in the family home and certainly lightened and enlivened the atmosphere. He constantly told jokes and played with his younger siblings. But he still found it difficult to get on with his father. Fishel scorned the religious traditions and wore a smart, modern hat and, like Shloime, had shaved off his side-locks and beard.

Fishel was not interested in getting married and settling down and soon became disenchanted with the traditional way of life in Mukačevo. In 1936, when faced with the prospect of compulsory army service, he left the family home again, without a word, in case his father or mother tried to dissuade him. He headed first to Belgium, where he took up employment on a ship, and it was on this ship that he managed to smuggle himself into America and avoid the catastrophe that befell Europe. He did not see Zisi again until some years after the war was over. By then, he was a changed man. The older Fishel, who was reunited with his surviving family members in the 1950s, was on the surface still as good-humoured and jovial as he had been in his youth, but he was clearly marked by sadness at the fate of his family, and guilt at having left them and being unable to do anything to rescue or help them. This was a burden that never left him.

6

All over Eastern Europe, younger Jews were turning to Zionism
as the way forward for the Jewish people

Among Zisi's most vivid early memories were the visits of her sister, Ruchel, 16 years her senior. Ruchtu, as she was known by her sisters, the second oldest girl in the Düm family, was blonde, beautiful and talented. Although Zisi barely remembered living under the same roof as her, she clearly recalls hearing about the time Ruchtu entered a beauty contest against her parents' wishes. She won, of course. She also learned of the misfortune of Ruchtu's first love. A young man named Keider came weekly to the house to teach the girls music, during which time Ruchtu and Keider developed a deep affection for each other. Keider's visits became more and more frequent until it was finally agreed that they could marry. Unfortunately, one day Ruchtu's elder brother Shloime saw Keider entering the local brothel. As soon as Shloime reported this to his family, the engagement was broken and a new husband sought for the heartbroken Ruchtu.

Thus it was that, at 19, she was betrothed to a man from Szatmárnémeti, known by the Jewish population as Satmar, about 70 miles from Mukačevo, in Hungarian Transylvania. His name was Mayer Katzenelbogen and his family owned a wine shop. Having joined her husband there, Ruchtu's life was not a particularly happy one. Mayer worked very hard and Ruchtu had to live with her mother-in-law who was not an easy woman to get on with. Despite giving birth to two sons, Ruchtu never felt at home in Satmar and very often came back to see her family in Mukačevo, usually with her two sons, Ushi and Fishi. Back among her own family, Ruchtu's happy, vibrant nature would restore itself and she brought much joy, laughter and song into the household, with the added bonus for Zisi that she got to know her older sister and to build a strong bond with her nephews.

Sari and Eti were only a couple of years apart in age and were always competing over clothes and other sisterly issues. Sometimes, after an argument, they would refuse to speak to each other for a couple of days. They were very different in character; Sari was more like her sister Ruchtu, impulsive, talented and lively. She was a particularly gifted dancer and singer and would have been a fine actress if custom had allowed it. She was extremely ambitious for herself and decided that she wanted to pass her matriculation exams and possibly go to university – an unusual path for girls at that time and one certainly not encouraged by the religious community.

Nevertheless, with the encouragement of her mother and despite the disapproving looks – but secret pride – of her father, Sari spent many hours studying when not helping in the shop. Her role in the shop was invaluable, on account of her strong sense of style and chic. She occasionally travelled with her father to Budapest to buy textiles and he sensibly tended to defer to her good taste. She and Ruchtu, in particular, were largely responsible for making both shop and home colourful and lively places.

When Eti left the home with her new husband in 1934, Sari took on the role of oldest sister, exercising her authority over the younger siblings. This led to many petty arguments with the younger children, as they tried to resist her forceful personality. But Sari was inevitably able to end the tension by making the others laugh and getting them to sing.

In 1942, at the age of 28, Sari married a man from Kosice called Erno Berkovits and left Mukačevo to build a family with him in Kosice. Soon after, they wrote to the family to announce Sari's pregnancy and in 1943 she gave birth to a daughter, Miryam-Rivka. When Kosice was occupied by the Germans in 1944, they managed to obtain false identity papers, leave Kosice and survive the war in Budapest, living as Christians.

Malchi was the sister closest in age (six years) to Zisi and the two of them formed a close friendship. They had their own friends but very much enjoyed each other's company and spent a great deal of time together, particularly in their early years. Malchi liked to read and to study. Her organisational and writing skills were such that she would often be involved in writing the family correspondence, notably when they needed to fill out forms and questionnaires. Not that any of this prevented her from being very helpful around the house.

Malchi often acted as peacemaker when arguments broke out at home. Like Zisi, she loved playing with friends in the street and picking green plums, apricots and cherries from the trees. She also enjoyed gymnastics at Sokol, the town's social club.

As a teenager, Malchi became involved in a Zionist youth movement called Hanoar Hatzioni. Her parents knew little of this activity but what they did know they were not happy about. Zionism was largely a secular, political movement, and though Hanoar Hatzioni was not anti-religious and respected the custom of girls and boys congregating separately, Zionist activities were not welcomed by her parents' generation.

On the other hand, all over Eastern Europe, younger Jews were turning to Zionism as the way forward for the Jewish people. With Europe in chaos, and its peoples at the mercy of constantly changing regimes and cruel Nazi domination, even without knowing of the horrors that lay ahead, these young Zionists believed there was a necessity and indeed an obligation for Jews to return to the Land of Israel and determine their own fate. Malchi, like many other members of Hanoar, hoped to find a way to make *aliyah* – to "go up", meaning to settle in Palestine – and, in preparation, she took classes in modern Hebrew.

In 1942, soon after Sari had left home, Malchi was introduced to Shimon Bernstein (Shimi), who was also from Mukačevo. In the same year, they were married and Malchi left the family home to live in another part of town. Six weeks later, Shimi was one of a large number of young Jewish men conscripted into the forced labour battalion, Munkatabor. Malchi remained alone in her new home receiving word from time to time from Shimi and spending increasingly long periods of time with her parents and Zisi in the family home.

Moishe, three years older than Zisi, was the youngest of the Düm boys. When Zisi was a small girl, she and Moishe were devoted playmates – she liked to wear his shirts – but, as they grew up, their views diverged dramatically. Moishe became very studious. Always a traditionalist, and devoutly religious, he also developed strong, right-wing tendencies that clashed directly with Zisi's left-wing views. Both believed in the Zionist dream of creating a homeland for the Jews in Palestine but they argued bitterly as to the nature of that homeland.

Chay-Adel felt particularly tender towards her youngest son, which seemed to arouse great jealousy in her husband, leading him to take an aggressive attitude towards Moishe. Eventually, Elazar's hostility drove his youngest son away from home, just as it had his brothers. One morning in 1937, when Moishe left without a word and did not return from morning prayers, Chay-Adel realised immediately that he had left. She went to the cupboard and discovered that all of Moishe's clothes were gone.

He wrote to his mother and sisters frequently from Belgium, where he told them that he was enjoying his studies. Two years later, he returned to a very different Mukačevo. His homecoming was short-lived, however. In 1941, like many of the young Jewish men from Mukačevo, Moishe was taken to serve in the forced labour battalion.

7

'Go, go read a little with Chaya'

Such were the words of Zisi's mother, Chay-Adel, encouraging her youngest daughter to go and spend time with another Chaya – Chaya Friedman, the daughter of a left-wing Zionist, non-religious cobbler. Despite her own deeply religious beliefs and the customary division between wealthy, religiously observant families and secular Zionist leftists, Chay-Adel always encouraged her daughters to expand their minds. While she knew that Zisi was reading texts and writers forbidden within religious circles, she understood that her daughter needed to prepare herself for a new society, one that expounded modern principles of Socialism and new, secular philosophies.

At six o'clock on Shabbat mornings, when the town was still very quiet, Zisi and her friend Chaya would steal away from their beds and walk down to the river bank, copies of Socrates, Plato and Hegel under their arms. There, by the river, they would walk past the inviting benches at the water's edge and carry on to a spot where the river narrowed and the water became shallow. Stepping carefully from rock to rock, they could reach a small, grassy island in the centre of the river. Here, they would sit and begin their intense discussion of worldly issues and life's challenges, stopping from time to time to read further passages from their chosen text before resuming their philosophical conversation. To anyone passing, it would have been a strange sight to observe these two young ladies alone in the middle of the river, engaged in such passionate debate. For the girls themselves it was a special time, imbuing them with self-confidence and affording them a mental stimulus.

On other occasions, Zisi and Chaya would go together to study piano at a local convent. Again encouraged by Zisi's mother, who would give Zisi money to pay for these lessons, the two girls progressed from piano at the convent to violin lessons from a young Jewish man who was to become a welcome visitor in Chaya's enlightened home. Chaya's family were all gifted musicians and Chaya had grown up learning the mandolin. She was thrilled to add piano and violin to her repertoire. For a girl like Zisi, from a religious home, having music lessons would normally be frowned upon at the very least, and she benefited greatly in this respect from her friendship with Chaya, especially when Chaya agreed to teach her to play the mandolin.

The two friends were both possessed of an adventurous and inquisitive nature, and were always keen to try new things. What was forbidden to Zisi by her religion was forbidden to Chaya by her family's income, obstacles that together they were well-equipped to overcome.

They had first met at the age of 13 at a meeting of the Zionist Socialist youth movement, Hashomer Hatzair (The Young Guard), in 1937. Zisi's involvement, with Chaya, in this political atmosphere at such a young age proved to be socially, emotionally and intellectually satisfying. Every Saturday evening after Shabbat, she would attend the meetings (*sichot*) where talks and debates took place about Zionism, Communism and Socialism, often featuring speakers from other towns. She became exposed to Marxist and other left-wing material and it all helped her to forge an individual Jewish identity very different from the traditions of her home and family. Zisi and her friends believed strongly in the principles of Zionism and made a point of taking on modern Hebrew names. And so at the age of 14 her Hashomer friends began to call her "Metouka" (Hebrew for sweet) in preference to the Yiddish.

At home, Zisi spoke little of her involvement with Hashomer Hatzair and, while her mother and father undoubtedly knew and disapproved of such a left-wing, non-religious movement, they were by then well accustomed to their children's rebellions. Each of Zisi's brothers and sisters rebelled in their own way. For Malchi, it was through belonging to Hanoar Hatzioni, another Zionist youth movement, though less radical than Hashomer Hatzair. Moishe joined the right-wing, religious Zionist group, Betar. Other siblings took up the contemporary fashions and ideals, notably in the way they looked and dressed or, in the case of the older boys, left home altogether.

The rise of Marxism and the Russian Revolution had a great effect on the young Jews of Eastern Europe, as did the emergence of political Zionism at the end of the 19th century. The early Jewish Socialists were powerfully attracted by Russian Socialism and its leaders, and followed the teachings of Karl Marx. For some, this meant the rejection of religion completely and the belief in universal Socialist principles. For others, such as those in the Russian-Lithuanian "Bund" Socialist movement, what was important was the development of a specific, Russian-Jewish-Socialist identity incorporating the Yiddish language.

By contrast, the Zionism of many Jews – on the right, the left and those not politically affiliated – was shaped by the pogroms, in which Jewish communities were looted and families attacked on a routine basis with Jews constantly being evicted from their homes and villages. This created a yearning to leave Eastern Europe – and Russia in particular – and "return" to the biblical homeland in Palestine. Despite the widespread support among young and progressive Jews in Eastern Europe for this manifestation of Zionism, orthodox rabbis saw it as an affront to their teachings. For them, the dream of the promised land, a homeland for Jews, was to be fulfilled only with the coming of the Messiah. Any thoughts of inhabiting the land of Israel before this biblical phenomenon were considered dangerous and anti-religious.

Mukačevo contained a range of Jewish youth movements across the political spectrum, Betar, Hanoar Hatzioni and Hashomer Hatzair being the main groupings. Betar believed in total Jewish control of Palestine, to which both Hashomer Hatzair and the more mainstream Hanoar Hatzioni were bitterly opposed. These two movements argued that Jews could share the land of Israel with the current inhabitants. In particular, Hashomer members believed they could find cultural and spiritual fulfilment only by building a new collective society in *Eretz Israel* (Land of Israel). Hashomer's members saw themselves as revolutionaries building a collective, based on Socialist principles enshrining the good of the group, as opposed to the individual. Both affluence and religion were scorned

In addition to the political activities of Hashomer, Zisi was introduced to various exciting new physical pursuits. Along with her Hashomer colleagues, Zisi decided to try her hand at skiing. Using money that her mother had given her with the express purpose of trying new activities, Zisi bought some fabric and secretly made herself some trousers – a garment that would never be countenanced for a modest religious girl – and she and Chaya took a bus to the outskirts of town in order to go skiing. They arrived at their destination, a hilly spot where skiing took place, rented some skis and, without knowledge or instruction, made their first attempt. Neither had any idea how to balance on skis and they both spent most of the time on their backsides, laughing loudly. But this did not deter them and Zisi joined other members of Hashomer Hatzair on short ski trips. She also enjoyed day trips to the countryside that were never too long to make her parents worry but were an exciting departure from normal religion and commerce-based life.

Through Hashomer, Zisi made a number of close friendships – including with young men. In her own religious community, teenage girls and boys did not mix together anywhere near as freely. Zisi enjoyed close friendships with two young men in particular: Moishe and Shlomo, both sons of religious families. Moishe was the brother of Rivka Klein, one of Zisi's class-mates. His family was well known to the Düm family and his considerable practical skills caused Zisi's father to overlook the usual custom where a girl did not bring a boy home. Moishe carried out various repairs in the Düm home and set up an electric lamp for Zisi's father to be able to read into the night.

Zisi, therefore, already had much in common with the two boys. But they were all keen Socialist Zionists and, together with Chaya, formed an inseparable foursome. They all loved to meet at Chaya's home, where they felt welcome, free and inspired. Chaya's mother, Mathilda Friedman, was a warm and intelligent woman who worked hard running the family vegetable stall in the central market. Chaya's father, Yaakov Friedman, made and mended shoes in a corner of the living room. The Friedmans' modest trade belied their deep knowledge of literature and politics. The five Friedman children all attended the modern and progressive Hebrew gymnasia, learning modern Hebrew and Zionist studies in addition to traditional Jewish studies. By the time Zisi befriended Chaya, the two older brothers had recently left home to study in Prague but on her visits to Chaya's home, Zisi also befriended her sisters, Rachel and Ada.

Zisi, Chaya, Moishe and Shlomo enjoyed lengthy discussions and ar-guments with Chaya's father, fondly known as *Friedman Batchi*, as well as numerous intellectual visitors to their two-room apartment. Friedman Batchi would frequently discuss Socialist issues with his guests as he made or repaired customers' shoes.

During these teenage years, Chaya's home became a second home to Zisi. Not only did she practise music there and participate in lively political debate, but she also watched Yaakov carefully as he stretched and sewed leather, fixed new heels, soles, buckles and laces to repair the old and create new footwear. Neither he nor Zisi could have known how important his trade would be in her survival.

8

*Her friend Kurt shouted at her, telling her to step off the pavement
and that Jews were only allowed to walk in the road*

Zlsi remembers sitting at her desk in school at the age of ten and, having
written the date and the year – 1934 – at the top of her page, looking out
of the window at her sister Gizi's fur shop across the road and smiling. She
recalls being happy at that time. With friendly Czech teachers serving under
the benign Czech rule, school was stimulating and enjoyable. Five years
later, early in 1938, she was sitting in exactly the same place when one of
her teachers pointed to Gizi's shop and said: "Now we will be free and really
develop and study. We shall not have any Jews looking over our shoulders."

By then, Mukačevo had been returned to Hungarian rule. When the
Czech President, Tomas Masaryk, died in 1937, his humanitarian liberal
rule died with him. Czechoslovakia became a loose federation and the area
was given autonomous status. In November 1938, in response to threats
from Germany and Hungary, intensive negotiations between Hungary and
Czechoslovakia resulted in the First Vienna Award under which some of the
land taken from Hungary under the 1920 Treaty of Trianon was returned.

The Vienna Award, supported by Italy and Germany, returned Mukačevo
and the southern part of Subcarpathian Rus' to a German-Hungarian alli-
ance. For Britain, France and Russia this was seen, naively, as a small price
to pay to prevent war. For Germany, it was just the beginning of a plan to
gain control of Europe with Hungarian and Italian support. For the Jews
of Mukačevo and the surrounding area, this was the beginning of dramatic
changes to their lives.

The installation of a Czech regime to the region in 1918 had brought
with it the Czech language, official recognition of the Jews as a distinct
minority with freedom of expression, and a generally liberal education in
the schools. The changes introduced in 1938 were instigated under a new,
much stricter regime. Public expression of left-wing politics was banned, as

was the fraternising of young men and women in public. Laws discriminating against Jews were also introduced.

From 1938, students no longer studied in Czech but in Hungarian. Boys and girls were now taught separately and discouraged from socialising together. New teachers were brought in to uphold the new school rules and where old ones were allowed to remain in their post, a marked change came about in their attitude to Jews.

The 1938 changes were disastrous for the Jews of Mukačevo. Discriminatory laws already in place in other areas of Hungarian rule now became operative in Mukačevo. Numerus Clausus, introduced in other areas of Hungary in 1920, restricted the number of Jews in higher education to six per cent. In July 1938, the First Jewish Law was introduced, limiting to 20 per cent the proportion of Jews allowed to work in the professions and in commerce and industry.

In Mukačevo the Jews who had been loyal to the democratic values of the Czech regime were condemned by non-Jewish inhabitants of the town, who publicly demonstrated their allegiance to Nationalistic Hungarian rule – and their approval of the anti-Jewish Laws. Some Jews did support the Hungarians, persuading themselves that their new masters' repressive measures were a strategy to placate their German Allies and avoid German interference as well as an attempt to prevent the fascist Arrow Party from gaining support.

This became a rare and increasingly blinkered line to take, however, once the Second Jewish Law was passed in 1939 defining Jews on racial grounds and restricting their numbers in intellectual professions, public sector employment, industry and commerce to six per cent.

After her teacher's anti-Semitic outburst in 1938, directed at Gizi's shop, Zisi and her Jewish friends found school life very difficult. Prior to 1938, the teachers had been respectful towards their Jewish pupils. Now they subjected them to overt discrimination. Jewish students were often separated in class; social activities were planned on Friday evenings thereby excluding religious Jews, who needed to be at home to welcome in the Sabbath.

As the teachers began to praise nationalism and express admiration for anti-Semitism, rules were gradually established making it compulsory for Jews to wear yellow badges and preventing them from being out after 6pm – and from walking on the pavement.

Until this point, Jewish and non-Jewish students had studied together happily. While there was not an enormous amount of interfaith mixing, Zisi did have non-Jewish friends. Now, gradually, she noticed these same friends behaving differently towards her. At first, her friend Trudi continued to sit next to her at school and made an effort to meet her outside school. But as time passed they saw less of each other, and Trudi was instructed by the teacher not to sit with Zisi. Kurt, who used to carry Zisi's books home for her at the end of school, was nowhere to be seen.

But, one afternoon, Zisi was walking home from her grandfather's house when she came across a group of non-Jewish boys, and Kurt was among them. She went to greet him but immediately stopped herself as she saw his frowning face. He then shouted at her, telling her to step off the pavement and that Jews were only allowed to walk in the road, so that she should know her place. Shocked, Zisi wondered what had possessed her friend to behave in such a manner. Was he protecting her from his friends by moving her out of the way? Was he perhaps also protecting himself from any violence that might follow if the other boys guessed that they were friends? She could not allow herself to believe that her good friend could turn on her in this fashion.

By 1941, public acts of anti-Semitism were not merely tolerated but encouraged by the authorities. The Third Jewish Law came in, prohibiting intermarriage and banning Jews from owning businesses, attending school or university or holding public office.

In anticipation of such measures, Zisi's father had already been approached by a man called Solontoy, a non-Jew who lived across the road from the shop. Following the Second Jewish Law, two years earlier, he and Elazar had agreed to transfer ownership of the shop into Solontoy's name. The two men reached an understanding that Solontoy would work in the shop and receive a salary but the profits would remain with the Düm family. As Zisi was under the age of 21, and no longer at school, she was allowed to work and so worked alongside Solontoy and his wife, representing her family's interests. With assistance from Elazar, Gizi entered into a similar arrangement regarding her fur shop with a trusted employee called Mutash. Behind the scenes, Elazar continued purchasing fabrics and advising Gizi, while Chay-Adel and Gizi continued doing the accounts from home.

9

*She took great care to cover all her books in case she was
stopped and searched in the street*

Working in the shop without her sisters became much more of a chore for
Zisi. The shop was no longer the same happy place. With no employment,
the vast majority of the Jewish population had little or no money to spend.
Moreover, because of the danger of anti-Semitic attacks, they would ven-
ture out on to the streets as little as possible. To alleviate the boredom, Zisi
would often bring in books to read and Chaya and other friends would
often come and visit Zisi at the shop. But the town-hall clock remained the
focus of her attention as she waited for closing time at 7 o'clock.

Solontoy was true to his word and for some months the Düm family
continued to live prosperously and remain in control of their store. However, towards the end of 1942, he died and his wife, known by the family as
Solontoyneni (Aunt Solontoy), took over. She was advised by her lawyers
to change the arrangement and instead of receiving a salary she took the
profits and paid the Düm family a salary as long as Zisi continued to work
with her in the store. The Düm family store no longer belonged to them;
they had no control and no real income and received no compensation for
the loss of their store and their livelihood.

From the early 1940s, the Hungarian authorities began conscripting all
young Jewish men into the forced labour battalions overseen by the army.
Most notably, these units were sent to help the war effort against Russia.
Consequently, by the end of 1942, there were no Jewish men between the
ages of 18 and 40 left in Mukačevo. Zisi's brothers, Shloime and Moishe,
and her brothers-in-law were all conscripted in the early 1940s. Her father,
who was in his mid-fifties, was considered too old and was therefore the
only male remaining at home. Young women such as Zisi were left to look
after the family, both old and young, and find a way to make ends meet.

Luckily for the Düm family, money was not such a problem and so the financial hardship was not so great but for many families this was a slow death sentence, as they had no savings and, without a livelihood, they were unable to feed their families. There were several particularly poor families on Zisi's street and, during this period, Zisi's mother, despite her own poor health, would send her daughter to deliver food and money more frequently than before.

Zisi was particularly concerned for her dear friend Yitte, whose father, Nachum the baker, had left some months earlier for the United States promising to send tickets for the rest of the family to join him once he had earned enough money. But, after a year, they had still heard nothing from him, and so it was left to Yitte and her younger brother Herman to try to earn some money by selling bread within the community. Yitte was often unable to help her brother as she suffered from tuberculosis and eventually was sent away to a sanatorium for several weeks. After she had returned, Zisi's mother encouraged Zisi to take butter and milk to the family regularly. Zisi also took remnants of fabric from the shop while Solontoyneni was not looking, which she gave to Yitte to make new clothing.

Despite the dangers posed by belligerent non-Jews on the streets, Zisi was undeterred from meeting her friends, going to Hashomer meetings and continuing her life as normal. The attraction of Hashomer had always been its Socialist, Zionist, non-religious outlook; from 1939, another significant attraction emerged – the sense of rebellion against the new Hungarian authorities. Whereas, under Czech rule, Socialism could be discussed and even openly encouraged, under the Hungarians it was forbidden. At first, left-wing organisations were simply disapproved of but in time they were banned. So, after the Hungarians took control in 1939, Zisi had to hide her attendance at Hashomer not merely from her parents, but more generally. Freedoms, especially for Jews, were being eroded. Jewish gatherings after dark were forbidden and all Socialist groups were outlawed. By 1940, the meetings of Hashomer were outlawed and Zisi and her friends met in secret. They could no longer use the Hashomer clubhouse but had to search for new meeting places and to move from one to the next from week to week. Members would spend days looking for new premises, examining lofts and cellars until they found rooms of an appropriate size to contain all the members. Meeting times and places were then passed on secretly by word of mouth, so as not to alert parents or the authorities.

With the works of Karl Marx and other left-wing books and pamphlets also forbidden, literature had to be smuggled into meetings and books were given bogus covers to disguise them. Zisi took great care to cover all of her books in case she was stopped and searched in the street. In spite of these difficulties, "illicit" youth movements continued to meet and members continued to read Marx and Lenin and discuss the burning social and political issues of the day. Although emissaries from Palestine were no longer allowed to lead these groups, the groups took on a life of their own and Zisi and her friends remained resolute and committed.

Around this time, she spent more and more time with Shlomo, Moishe and Chaya at Hashomer meetings and in Chaya's home in deep discussion with Chaya's family and their visitors. On the day of a meeting, Zisi took care not to arrive at the same time as her friends and they all ensured that they were not seen walking together. They would leave the gatherings separately and meet up later, often at Chaya's house. Despite the dangers to Jews out on the streets, particularly after curfew, Moishe and sometimes Shlomo would invariably escort Zisi home.

At Chaya's house, however, things were becoming increasingly difficult. Chaya's father, who had suffered from stomach ulcers for several years, was recovering from an operation and his health was very poor. While unofficially he was able to continue his work, catering to friends and neighbours, physically he struggled and, by 1943, he was no longer able work at all.

Chaya's mother, Mathilda, was no longer allowed to run her market stall and so the family were dependent on the little work that she and her three daughters could do and on the small amount of family savings. Chaya's brother, who was studying medicine in Prague, sent them money from time to time and they managed to struggle on.

In late 1943, after several months of ill health following his operation, Yaakov, Chaya's father, passed away. The news reached Zisi the same day and, as she prepared to run over to Chaya's house to comfort her, Zisi's mother called her and told her to go via the shop and take enough white cloth to cover Yaakov's body for burial. When Zisi arrived at Chaya's home, Chaya's mother was overcome with grief and gratitude for this significant offering without which they would not have been able to bury her husband in a dignified fashion.

The loss of Yaakov was felt by many, remembering his open house where people would come to discuss the great matters of the day; remembering, too, his great belief in the future of the Jewish people, in Zionism and Socialism. All this served as an inspiration to many – including Zisi.

10

Her premature death meant that she did not have to contend with
the murder of her husband, four children and all ten grandchildren

As the war years continued, life in Mukačevo grew increasingly harsh, especially for its Jewish population. Zisi found herself stretched in several directions. During the day, she continued to work in the store, excusing herself early so that she could help her sister Gizi. With her husband taken away to the forced labour battalion, Gizi was struggling with four children and Zisi's company provided a pleasant distraction for the children and relief for Gizi herself. Chay-Adel's health remained poor and consequently she spent much more time resting at home. And, when Zisi returned from Gizi's or from working at the shop, she would take over from her father or her sister Malchi the duties of caring for her mother.

Zisi would spend several hours reading to her mother in Yiddish. Although Yiddish was spoken in the home, Zisi was the only one who could read Yiddish fluently and her mother would particularly enjoy Zisi reading to her as it helped her to relax and sleep through the night.

With her family needing her so much, Zisi could not devote as much time as she had in the past to Hashomer Hatzair activities but she still made sure that she attended meetings and met her friends whenever she could.

Zisi's sisters Sari and Malchi were both betrothed and married in the same year, 1942. Sari went with her husband Erno to live in his home town of Kosice and Malchi also left the family home to live with her new husband, Shimon "Shimi" Bernstein. By the end of that year, Zisi was the only daughter still living at home and her father Elazar and grandfather David Schlussel were the only male members of the Düm family left in Mukačevo. The younger men were all in the labour battalions. As a result, the women were left to earn a livelihood and manage their families alone.

Shloime's wife, Sara, was alone in their Kosice home with a new baby and a small child. For a period during that significant year of 1942, Zisi's mother's health improved somewhat and Zisi was sent to Kosice to help Sara for a few weeks. Zisi – who loved small children – was very happy to be with her sister-in-law, and she and Sara, fondly known as Surchu, formed a close bond.

While Zisi happily spent a month with Surchu, she was relieved to return home to see how her mother was doing and how her friends Yitte and Chaya and their families were managing.

Zisi and her parents became particularly anxious about the lack of word from her beloved elder sister Eti and her family in faraway Topolchani. From late 1942, Eti's letters and visits ceased and they heard no more from her. Rumours emerged that the Jews of the Topolchani area had been deported to labour camps but the Düm family back in Mukačevo could find out nothing. Zisi's mother was desperate with worry and would cry out for Eti in her sleep.

They did, however, continue to hear from Sari and Erno in Kosice, who were able to tell them that they were well and that Sari was expecting a baby. On the other hand, Malchi's marital happiness was short-lived – six weeks after their wedding, her bridegroom Shimi was conscripted into the dreaded labour battalion. A few months later in early 1943, Malchi decided to return to live in the family home with Zisi and her parents, her spirits raised every time she received a letter from Shimi.

By mid-1943 Chay-Adel's health and spirits were slowly deteriorating, however. Despite the happy news of the birth of a daughter, Miryam Rivka, to Sari and Erno in Kosice, they had not heard from Eti and her family for more than a year. Meanwhile, Eti's sisters, Gizi, Malchi and Ruchtu, were all having to manage the uncertainty of life without their husbands. The Düm sons, Shloime and Moishe, were both far away in the ranks of the forced-labour recruits, with only the infrequent letter proving that they were still alive. And rumours were circulating among the youth movements and on the radio about the privation and cruelty prevailing in the concentration camps. Nevertheless, the Düm family defiantly clung on to hope.

During this time, Ruchtu returned from Satmar to join Zisi and Malchi in the family home. Concerned for her mother's health and with her husband in the forced-labour units, Ruchtu decided to bring her sons Ushi and Fishi back to Mukačevo. Ruchtu's lively presence gave the family a welcome boost and Zisi was especially happy to have the company of the two young boys. During the day, Zisi continued to take her place in the shop while Malchi and Ruchtu looked after things at home and, in the evenings, Zisi would return and take over the care of her mother.

Zisi did manage occasionally to get out of the demanding domestic routine and although the Hashomer Hatzair meetings were now rather infrequent, she did see Chaya whenever she could. It was not like old times, as their contact was frequently limited to a short visit by Chaya to the Düm store and then a hurried departure so as not to be caught by the evening curfew.

In the winter of 1943, Chay-Adel's health took a sudden turn for the worse with the onset of pneumonia. Elazar and his daughters took turns to try to nurse her back to health but, without antibiotics, it was an uphill struggle. Every night, Zisi would return from work and continue the Yiddish readings to her mother – which comforted both of her parents as, by then, Elazar would also sit and listen.

But Chay-Adel's health continued to deteriorate. One night, Zisi returned from work to find Ruchtu and her father in an extremely anxious state, and Chay-Adel struggling for breath with a soaring temperature. Zisi and Ruchtu risked violating the curfew to look for a doctor. Several doctors whom they approached were too afraid to come out, but eventually they each returned accompanied by a doctor. Both doctors confirmed what the family had feared – without medication, Chay-Adel was unlikely to survive.

All that the family could do was watch Chay-Adel slowly suffocate, with the one consolation of having three of her children by her side. Zisi remembers how fearful she was of coming home to find her mother struggling for breath, so that one night, when she returned home from work in January 1944 and found her mother no longer suffering, she was at first relieved. It was only when, early next morning, she saw her mother's body being washed and prepared for burial that the terrible reality hit her and she started screaming for the loss of her darling mother.

Later that day, Zisi, Malchi, Ruchtu and Gizi buried their mother in the Jewish cemetery in Mukačevo. Their father was a Cohen – of priestly descent – and therefore, under Jewish law, not allowed to enter the cemetery, so he was consoled at home by his grandchildren. At the funeral, despite the warnings against large gatherings, Zisi felt comforted by the large presence of well-wishers from all over town, many crying over their own misfortune at losing a woman who had made life a little easier for them with her constant help and kindness.

At home, after the funeral, the family observed the traditional seven days of *shiva* (mourning), almost speechless with their loss. On the second day, Zisi's brother Moishe arrived home, after managing to gain a transfer from one work-camp to another. His joy at seeing his sisters again was obliterated by the shock of learning of his mother's death. Moishe's visit remains in Zisi's memory as a deeply distressing event, when few words were spoken before he had to leave again for another work detail.

Elazar's grief at losing his wife was great; his tears softened his daughters' accumulated anger toward him. In the months that followed, Elazar saw very few people, except when praying in the synagogue, and quietly devoted himself to his books.

After several months, Ruchtu decided to leave Mukačevo and return to her mother-in-law's house in Satmar. Despite their difficult relationship, Ruchtu's sense of duty encouraged her to go back in the hope that the two women would help each other through the hard times. She took with her just one of her sons, Ushi, leaving Fishi in Zisi's care. If things improved in Satmar, she would return for him. Zisi was delighted to have the 12-year-old Fishi in the house and indeed the boy proved to be a comforting presence for the stricken Elazar and for Gizi and her children.

In later years, the surviving Düm children came to regard Chay-Adel's premature death as a blessing. As a mother, she did not have to witness the suffering of her children, nor did she have to contend with the murder of her husband, four children and all ten grandchildren. For Zisi today, this consolation is qualified by a sense of injustice that such a righteous woman should have suffered such a painful death and be denied the legacy of leaving her children and grandchildren to what should have been a healthy and fulfilled life.

11

With a heavy heart and tears pouring down her cheeks, she wrote
a short note: "To those that use this house, I hope you will be as
happy as I was here"

Zisi, Malchi, their father and young nephew Fishi, Ruchtu's son, celebrated the Passover Seder of 1944 alone. It was too late and too dangerous for Gizi and her children to join them. Suddenly, the peace of the night was disturbed by the thud of soldiers' marching footsteps and loud singing: *"Zsido, rohadt zsido. Mit keresel itt?"* ("Jew, bloody Jew, what are you doing here?").

In spite of this, Elazar Düm insisted on opening the front door for Elijah and chanting the words to welcome any stranger that is hungry. *"Mi she raev"* ("He that is hungry").

The German army had entered Mukačevo on March 19, 1944. Very soon, the collective hatred of the citizens of Mukačevo, previously directed only at their severe Hungarian masters, was transferred to the German invaders. The Jewish community found itself in the ironic position of longing for the days of Hungarian rule. From the moment the Germans entered Mukačevo, the Hungarian militia, the Nilosh, worked together with the German authorities to terrorise the Jews into submission. Jews were beaten on the streets and forced at gunpoint to give up their valuables. Homes were raided. The leaders of the community urged people to submit to the authorities' demands in return for their lives. The Jews agreed, believing German reassurances that their compliance would be rewarded and secretly hoping that the Red Army would reach Mukačevo soon.

Zisi and her family tried their best to stay indoors and warned her father not to go out; bearded Jewish men were being stopped and beaten. She and Malchi were the only ones to step outside to try to buy food and to visit Gizi. But, within a few days, flyers were delivered to each household and posters displayed in public places, telling Jews to collect their belongings together and be ready to – "temporarily" – leave their homes. They were ordered to register their addresses, property and any remaining valuables with the authorities. On the other side of town, wooden fences were being hastily erected around two separate areas, one of which was where Zisi's friend Chaya lived. These enclosed areas were to become ghettos.

Then, notices were posted telling all the Jews of Mukačevo to pack up their things immediately, leave their homes and make their way to the ghetto areas. Zisi left her father, sister and nephew packing and made her way to Chaya's house on Koshut Street in the ghetto area and asked if she could bring her family to stay there. Even though Chaya's mother Mathilde Friedman was already sheltering members of her own family, she readily agreed to welcome Zisi's family into her two-room home. Zisi hurried back to her own house with the news that she had secured a place for the family to stay.

While Elazar and Fishi were busy packing, Zisi and Malchi decided to take their mother's jewellery and earrings, and some of their money, and find places in the cellar to hide it all. Underneath a large wooden box where potatoes were stored, they dug a hole in the earth and buried the jewellery and valuables. They then hid a few other items of value at different points around the cellar.

Eventually, with a suitcase under one arm and a straw mattress under the other, each of the four remaining members of the Düm family stepped out of the house into an almost empty street. As they carried on walking, their non-Jewish neighbours kept well out of the way, not wanting to show their faces. Most of the houses of their Jewish friends and neighbours were already locked up and silent. Before long, they were joined by hundreds of families laden with their belongings, all making their way to the far side of the town, and the supposed safety of the ghetto.

After seeing Elazar, Malchi and Fishi safely ensconced in Chaya's house, Zisi went back to the family home one more time, to gather as much food as she could carry. Remembering that she had a few gold coins at home, once she got there she quickly hid these in a small crevice by the window ledge in the cellar. She reasoned that the coins would probably be the first items of value to be found and hoped that, on discovering them, anyone looking for valuables would be satisfied and search no more. As she left, she took great care to close the heavy wooden shutters and secure the house. It was with a heavy heart and tears pouring down her cheeks that she wrote a short note, which she left on the dining room table:

"To those that use this house, I hope you will be as happy as I was here."

She then closed the front door and, without looking back, she exited the courtyard and made her way to join the rest of her family.

For three weeks, Zisi and her family, together with Chaya and members of her family, lived in two rooms in the Friedman household. The Düms had expanded to include Gizi and her two children who joined them two days after Zisi's arrival. During the day, the mattresses spread out on the floor acted as seats and at night they served as beds. The day was spent preparing food for this large number of people or standing outside and talking to others in the square opposite the apartment. There was no work or school and no organised activity was allowed. Food could be obtained only on the black market; otherwise the families had to exist on what they had brought with them.

Movement around the ghetto, although not restricted, was not always safe. The Nilosh would victimise the vulnerable; Zisi often witnessed older men having their beards cut off and younger men being beaten for trying to find food for their children. She managed to persuade her father to shave off his beard, insisting that he would be much safer. This was such a radical change that on one occasion she didn't realise that she was standing next to him outside, having completely failed to recognise him in his beardless incarnation.

Everyone in the ghetto was in a state of shock and it took some time for the inhabitants to make efforts to normalise life as far as was possible. The ghetto was awash with rumours. Radios were not allowed but some news did filter through. However, this was usually grim and unlikely to raise the spirits. Broadly speaking, younger inhabitants tried to lift the atmosphere by singing and joking, while their elders tried their best to overcome their circumstances by continuing to gather to pray and study in makeshift premises set in people's homes.

Zisi's clearest memory of this time is of the final evening in the ghetto. It was mid-May, and all the families had been told that they were to pack one bag each and appear in the square the next morning at 4am to be taken to work camps. Chaya and her sister Rachel sat with Zisi silently looking through the window at the empty night, filled with dread about what was going to happen just a few hours later.

By four o'clock in the morning, dressed in several layers of clothing to avoid having to carry so much, the ghetto residents stood outside their houses, bags packed and ready. They stood there for hours until eventually they were ushered by the Nilosh in rows of five through the gates and out of the ghetto.

It felt as though they were about to be marched in military fashion to whatever their immediate destination was. But it quickly became apparent that it was going to be even worse than marching. Once they were outside the ghetto, they were ordered in the rough voices of their captors to keep in the rows of five but to run. As they did so, many of their bags and suitcases fell open and their contents tumbled out to the ground.

The Nilosh yelled at them to keep running, despite the burden of the belongings that they were carrying. No mercy was shown towards anyone who stumbled; they were beaten with sticks until they pulled themselves up and continued running. If they were unable to do so, they would be left on the side of the street to die. At first, several people stopped to try and help others, pick them up and get them moving, but anyone helping also got beaten and so, slowly, those who fell were left to be beaten alone.

In Zisi's row she had her father on one side and Fishi on the other. She constantly put out her hands to protect her father and Fishi and received several blows to the arm, after which Fishi would take hold of her hand and kiss the place on her arm where she had been beaten.

Their route out of town took them down Bereksaz. Zisi choked back tears as they went past the Düm family home, which was already in ruins; the shutters that she had so carefully closed just three weeks ago were hanging open, some off their hinges, and the windows were smashed.

By this time, the running had been reduced to a rapid marching pace. For more than an hour, they continued along the five-kilometre route towards the brick works on the edge of town. But now its courtyard, where goods would be loaded on trains for delivery, was empty of bricks. Instead, hundreds of men, women and children were sitting or lying on the ground in small groups. Zisi and her family were ushered into a small area where they could set themselves and their belongings down and were given six bricks to mark their territory. Here, in the open on the bare ground, they would be made to remain for several days.

No sooner had they laid out their belongings and sat down to rest than the militia men came screaming orders at them again. The air was filled with tension. No one knew what to expect; every command came suddenly and aggressively without warning. They were told to give up all cash, jewellery and other valuables. Those who didn't comply would be shot. Shots were fired into the air and examples made of people whom their captors assumed – or randomly decided – were hiding something of value.

Many of these terrified and bewildered victims hastily removed their jewellery and gave it up to the militia. But when Elazar gave Zisi a large amount of cash, she rapidly hid it in her underwear. Then, she and a few others built a fire. Two of their number were assigned to act as guards as Zisi threw banknotes into the fire with some relief. Those that were not burnt in this way, she hid in a gap in a wall. They had already previously disencumbered themselves of their jewellery in their cellar in Bereksaz. So now they were left with nothing.

12

'That's your family up there in the smoke'

Food was sparse during the days at the brick factory. Zisi, Gizi and Malchi had all managed to bring some with them on the march out of the ghetto but it was barely enough to feed them all. Bowls of soup and water were passed round intermittently but, as the days drew on, hunger, rather than fear, became the prevailing anxiety.

Zisi and Chaya had become separated on the journey from the ghetto to the brick factory and Zisi was distressed not to be able to find her friend there. She did meet other friends and cousins, however, and spent many hours with them. Sitting with her classmate Shifra or with her cousins Zishka and Libshe, she even managed to relax and laugh. There was little serious talk of escape. In the absence of young men, the young women – many with children or older parents to care for – could not allow themselves to think about escape, which would mean abandoning their loved ones. Zisi mostly stayed close to her father, as well as to Fishi, Malchi and Gizi's children. Elazar barely spoke during this time and would often be seen sitting and praying together with other older men.

The combination of cold April nights, hard ground and the constant sound of trains made sleep difficult. Every day, a new trainload of Jews from the neighbouring villages would enter the station siding. It would remain there for hours while the unfortunate arrivals were kept inside the closed trucks through whose wooden slats those already in the brick factory could make out pleading eyes and hands. They could be heard crying out for help – and for water: *"Wasser, Wasser, a bisele Wasser!"*

Whenever a train approached, people from the brickyard tried to get close to the trains with food and water but were beaten back by the guards. On one such occasion, Zisi and Fishi tried crawling along the ground to reach the carriages, but they too were beaten back. Zisi felt a sense of relief when the crying and screaming finally stopped and the train left the station – but only to be replaced by another some hours later, bringing the same mournful cries for water.

After a week or so in the brick-factory yard, the arrival of a train had a different significance, for Zisi and her family were ordered at gunpoint to board it, along with hundreds of other Jewish prisoners. Grabbing their belongings, Zisi took hold of Fishi's hand and together with Malchi, Gizi, her children and her father they were herded into a carriage packed with about 100 people. There was no room to sit; everybody was squashed together upright. After several hours of standing with neither food nor water, while the train did not move, the children and older people took it in turns to sit down.

The train remained stationary for hours in the heat of the spring sunshine and it was hard to breathe. There was great relief when the train eventually started to move and they could feel the air blowing in through the wooden slats. There were many long stops along the route but, without windows and only small openings between the wooden planks, they were unable to identify where they were. From time to time, Zisi saw her nieces, Hava and Juditko stretching out their hands pleading for some food. Just a couple of months earlier this would have been a welcome gesture from Hava, a little girl who ate so little; here it just brought further anguish to Zisi's heart.

In the heat and the darkness, Zisi closed her eyes and tried to imagine she was back at home in Mukačevo. There was nothing else she could do; the whimpering of the small children and the moans of the old people of her carriage made it impossible to escape. With no toilets or sanitary facilities, other than a single bucket, the people in the truck designated one corner for their toileting needs. The stench over the course of what became a four-day journey was overwhelming and unavoidable. From time to time, the bucket was emptied through a hole in the wooden planks but, as the train gathered speed, the remains of urine and excrement flew back into their faces.

At one point, Zisi managed to fall asleep leaning against a wall. When she awoke, she found Fishi standing up and she found space for him on the floor so that he could sleep. The lack of food or water made the journey increasingly unbearable. One woman lost her mind and called out as they passed through various stations: "Is this Vienna? Is this Vienna? I must get out." And then, later: "Is this Paris? Is this Paris? Please let me out."

Along with this woman's constant, pathetically deluded pleadings, the babies in the truck cried incessantly. Zisi fought back wishful thoughts that the babies would just stop crying for good. She closed her eyes and, after a time, began to see a small, twinkling star in the darkness of her vision and managed to train herself to concentrate on this star, this Glimmer of Hope, in order to block out the noise. Had she known what lay ahead, she would have cared little about the cries of children.

She felt a brief sense of relief and hope as they pulled into a brightly lit station, with what appeared to be a large but well-organised welcoming party. The train remained stopped for a while and then Zisi's brief moment of optimism was ended by the all-too-familiar barking of orders. The carriage doors were flung open to the cries of *"Heraus! Heraus!"*. Shots were fired into the air as they were pulled off the train and pushed along the platform by young men and women, dressed in striped uniform, calling to them in Yiddish. If these people were Jews, the new arrivals thought, why were they being so unkind? Why were they so rough? Screams of terror filled the air, as people were beaten if they hesitated for a moment.

As they were pulled off the train and herded away, their bags were snatched away from them with no explanation. One of the Yiddish speakers pulling Zisi and her family from the train whispered to her: "You are in Auschwitz. Say they are 16," pointing to Fishi and Juditko. Others told her father: "Say you are a carpenter, say you have a trade. Give the young children to the old people, save yourselves." Neither the name of the station, Auschwitz II (Auschwitz-Birkenau), nor the warnings of those helping them off the train meant anything to them, they were too frightened and too tired to listen.

They stood in line waiting, surrounded by members of the SS. The queue of people inched forward until they came before a German officer sitting at a small table. He looked at the people and, with one finger, indicated where they should go. Zisi, Malchi, Gizi and her children were directed to the left, Fishi and Elazar to the right. While Zisi's heart pounded as Fishi and her father were sent in the opposite direction with all the men, Zisi was pleased that Fishi was with her father, thinking that Fishi would be able to look after him. But then Malchi and Zisi were once again ordered to go in a different direction to Gizi and the children. Bewildered by all these shouts and orders, Zisi gestured to Gizi to indicate that she would look for her later.

The air smelt of burning and dark smoke floated above them. Zisi asked one of the women in striped uniforms, who were still escorting the new arrivals, what the smell was. "That's your family up there in the smoke," was the reply. Zisi and Malchi thought she was deranged.

Again they were made to stand for several hours until they were sorted into groups. They were then taken to a building and told to remove their clothes. Despite the presence of male soldiers, Zisi ripped off her clothes for fear she would be beaten for not getting them off quickly enough. Out in the open and inhibited by their bodies and the cold of the morning, the women stood huddled together. One by one, they were approached by a burly female guard with a razor, who grabbed hold of their hair and shaved it off to the scalp. Every other inch of hair was shaved from their bodies. When this particular humiliation was over, Zisi panicked because she could not see Malchi. Then the naked, bald figure next to her called out her name. The two sisters looked at each other and fell into each other's arms, half-laughing at their ridiculous appearance and half crying from fear and relief.

Zisi's solitary comfort at that moment was that her dearest Malchi was by her side. Each girl was desperately afraid of losing the other. From that day in early May 1944, they were inseparable.

13

Zisi, wearing nothing but her black cocktail dress,
stood next to Malchi, in the freezing cold

Stripped naked, huddling together more from fear than cold, Zisi and Malchi were made to wait until everyone stood naked and shaven. Then, from having worn extra layers of clothing back in Mukačevo, the two sisters, along with the other new inmates, were each issued with a single garment that had previously belonged to another prisoner. Zisi was given a short, black, cocktail dress. These were just random allocations, irrespective of size, and whatever each prisoner was given would be the sole item of clothing she would wear, day and night, for the next few days until she received a prisoner's striped uniform.

Zisi and her companions presented a bizarre sight – a group of women of various shapes and sizes, hairless, in strange dresses that did not fit them. Now well and truly incarcerated, as they could see from the barbed-wire fences around the camp perimeter, Zisi and Malchi wandered around desperately trying to catch sight of other family members or friends.

Whenever they passed a group of prisoners behind barbed wire on the other side from them, Zisi would ask about family members, her father, Fishi and Gizi. She was particularly anxious about the children. If only she had said that Juditko was 16, perhaps her young niece would now be with them. The lack of information and the smell of the smoke sickened her to the stomach. Yet, she still had hope, as she could never believe that anybody could commit crimes of the scale and nature that were in fact happening in that place.

After several more aimless hours, they were given their first hot drink in several days – a form of coffee with a bitter taste that did not prevent them from consuming it eagerly. The bitter taste was caused by bromide, which the SS had put in the coffee to render the drinkers more docile and compliant. It also slowed down the body's activity so that they no longer menstruated. They would be given this bromide coffee at regular intervals. Once the women realised what the effects were and why it was being administered to them, Zisi, still trying to remain positive, argued that it at least helped the women keep clean.

Eventually, they were rounded up and marched towards a barrack building. They arrived beyond exhaustion, beyond fear, to be shown inside where there was an arrangement of bunk beds. Each bunk, bare and without a mattress, was allotted to between 10 and 12 women. When they lay down, squashed together in such a tight space, there was not enough room for them to stretch out or lie on their backs but the relief, after hours of standing and walking, was immense.

While it was somewhat comforting for Zisi to have the warmth of Malchi's body next to hers, she was unable to sleep. As she closed her eyes, she experienced a range of emotional images in her mind – of her home, her parents, the terrifying train journey, Fishi kissing her arm where the Nilosh had beaten her. She tried the technique she had invented in the train, focusing with her eyes closed on a twinkling star and did manage to fall into a fitful sleep.

At four o'clock in the morning, they were roused with cries from the female SS Guards – *"Heraus, Heraus, Schnell, Schnell"*. Then the Kapos – veteran prisoners who had been placed in charge of the newer arrivals, one Kapo to one group of prisoners – came and urged them to get out of bed immediately for roll-call. Exhausted, confused and frightened, Zisi and Malchi found themselves outside in the dark of the early morning, standing once again in one of many rows of five. They would become used to this routine, which took several hours to complete as it took in around 14,000 prisoners at a time.

Zisi, wearing nothing but her black cocktail dress, stood next to Malchi, in the freezing cold. Still confused about their situation, some of the new prisoners asked the veterans about their luggage and the smells in the smoky air. But it didn't take long for them to acclimatise to the hard reality. From time to time they were allowed to stroll about the camp in a confined area, where they would speak to other prisoners and ask after their loved ones again. The only answers they received deepened their distress.

Lunch was a piece of bread and some watery soup, again with that familiar bitter taste of bromide. In the evenings, there was a counting-in roll call and the inmates would once more have to stand waiting for hours before it was completed. And so, every day followed the same pattern, with the roll-call – *Appel* – the focal point. As the time for Appel approached, tension spread through the ranks of women. The SS were always looking to remove prisoners from the roll-call. Every morning, one or two prisoners would be selected, some were taken to carry out a particular task, others never returned. Every morning, Zisi and Malchi would stand together awaiting their fate. They tried to merge with the crowd and not draw attention to themselves to avoid being singled out. For the moment, luck remained on their side.

But Zisi was impatient and she wanted to talk to prisoners from other barracks to get some idea of what was going on in this grim and deadly camp. She often left the relative safety of the barrack during the day – despite warnings from Malchi and others – to take a walk in search of information. On one such occasion, an SS guard stopped her and told her that if she wanted to do some work in the kitchen she could earn herself some extra food. On other occasions, she found the strength to volunteer for cleaning duty and, to the amazement of her fellow inmates, she set to work immediately sweeping and washing the floors.

Approximately six weeks later, now wearing identical striped uniforms, Zisi and Malchi attended Appel for the final time at Auschwitz. On this particular morning, the SS started the familiar selection process, dividing the women into different groups. Fortunately, Malchi and Zisi were able to keep together. Also with them was their cousin Libshe and other friends from home but they were separated from their cousin, Zishka. They had no idea what they were being selected for but Zisi did have the idea that she would not be returning to the barrack that night.

Approximately a hundred women were marched out through the gates of Auschwitz, underneath the large arch that displayed the words: *Arbeit Macht Frei.* As they exited the gates, a band of female inmates, their shaven heads covered with red scarves, were playing on musical instruments and Zisi and her friends were ordered to sing: *"Es geht alles vorüber, es geht alles vorbei"* ("Everything will be over, everything will pass").

They now found themselves among many such groups of both men and women, each group wearing a different coloured headscarf. After several hours of waiting, they were marched off. Some of the prisoners were carrying tools, and were seemingly going to work. Others, including Zisi's group, were being herded towards a train, on to which, after further hours of waiting, they were ordered.

This, of course, immediately triggered memories of their previous, horrific train journey. This time, though, there was more room and Zisi and Malchi were both able to sleep on the floor. The train came to a halt in the darkness and the prisoners were all ordered from the train. They were marched to a new camp, where they were permitted to climb into their bunks and sleep.

By the morning, they had already learnt that they had been brought to Stutthof, a camp near Gdansk (Danzig) on the Polish German Border. This was notorious for the brutality inspired by its tyrannical commandant, Max Pauli, known as "Mad Max".

14

There seemed to be no end to the cruel games he invented

Although Max Pauli was no longer the commandant when Zizi arrived at Stutthof camp in June 1944, his brutal procedures continued under his successor Paul-Werner Hoppe. Many of the prisoners still referred to the new commandant as Mad Max. For example, when the inmates were given soup, outside the buildings, it would be in a scaldingly hot metal bowl. They were then ordered to run into the dining area, hands burnt from the metal bowl and the soup spilling everywhere before they arrived in their places. Anyone caught consuming soup outside would have their food confiscated and be given a beating.

Several of the guards seemed to take pleasure in the prisoners' suffering. At one point, the prisoners were given stale bread and forced to eat it outside in the midday sun. After several meals like this, many prisoners were unable to control their bowels. Then, with two thousand prisoners running for the toilets, the Commandant would order the closure of half of them. The consequent queues meant an intolerable wait but anyone who lost control – following constant checks by the guards – was beaten. Living up to his predecessor Mad Max's reputation, Hoppe's aggressive shouting and unpredictability made both prisoners and guards nervous. There seemed to be no end to the cruel games he invented.

By the end of July 1944, Zisi and Malchi were on the move again. Still together, they once more found themselves herded on to a train. After another long journey, the train arrived in, Bydgoszcz, named Bromberg by the Germans.

Here, the sisters were taken into another camp, known to them as Brannau, which by comparison with their experience so far of captivity under the Nazis, appeared almost a paradise. Inside their allotted block, Zisi and Malchi were directed to a bunk bed and told to share the upper part – and a blanket. In the morning, they were given milk to drink and newer striped uniforms. After roll-call, they were marched for two kilometres to a munitions factory.

There, they were put to work with prisoners of war from Belgium, Poland and Russia. Friendships and even romances were formed, despite the intimidating presence of Nazi guards. Each day, during the break period, these prisoners of war would teach the women how to sabotage the bombs that they were charged with manufacturing. Soon, Malchi and Zisi became experts. Standing alongside a conveyor belt, their job was to insert a metal rod securely in the middle of each device. But, when no one was watching, they would snap the middle piece of this rod, so that it could never detonate.

It was dangerous work; the explosives gave off poisonous fumes and the female prisoners were not allowed protective masks, unlike the POWs, who were issued with them. Zisi was constantly fearful of faulty detonators, or that one of the guards might spot her disabling a bomb. But she also gained considerable satisfaction from knowing that she was sabotaging the German war effort.

With a more organised routine, she and her fellow inmates at Brannau felt a little more secure, and even independent. Yoli, a large, tough Jewish prisoner, was selected by the SS as *Blockaltester* (manager of the block). Yoli took this responsibility seriously and kept the other prisoners strictly in line. In return, she received better living conditions, and better food, which she was able to share with her three sisters.

Although many of the women felt bitter resentment towards Yoli, Zisi befriended her. Yoli would often ask Zisi to explain to the other prisoners that her toughness and aggression was only a strategy to appease the ever watchful SS Guards. Even so, Zisi had difficulty reconciling Yoli's tough exterior, which could move her to strike a fellow Jew for not working hard enough, with her frequent kindnesses shown in giving extra milk and food to those who were sick.

These were mainly individuals suffering from malnutrition, infection and other illnesses brought on by their situation, which, though an improvement on what it had been before, was still perilous. Fortunately, some invalids were able to be treated in a small clinic by a Jewish doctor. Zisi attended the clinic with infected boils and blisters brought on by the poor working conditions, long marches to and from work and having to stand throughout 12-hour work shifts. She befriended the doctor, who showed her how to treat these conditions. Never one to sit around, when the clinic was very busy Zisi would help out by treating sore feet and minor health problems.

Zisi made numerous friends, chatting after work in and around the hut in which she and Malchi were based. She even managed to keep her brain active by teaching German to one fellow inmate who, in return, taught Zisi Hebrew.

A particular punishment favoured by the guards at Brannau was to make the women stand on a steep hill in the cold for several hours, usually positioned so that the wind was blowing in their faces. Determined not to just stand and watch, Zisi organised her fellow prisoners to crawl past the guards to give food or drink to those being punished. Even when she was caught trying to help one of her friends on the hillside and punished in the same way, it did not stop her continuing to organise ways to relieve these victims.

Although the clinic was available to help the prisoners with small injuries and health problems, for some women the hunger, cold and exhaustion brought on more complicated conditions. Zisi's cousin Libshe became very ill and, lacking proper medical care, died even though Malchi and Zisi brought her extra food. The guards agreed to allow Zisi and two other women to give the body a proper burial. Zisi and the others walked in front of the horse and cart that carried Libshe's body.

As they passed through a residential area, some people called out mockingly "*Oy veh, oy veh*," the well-known Yiddish expression of woe. When they arrived at the cemetery, the women were given shovels to dig the grave while the guards looked on. When they had finished their task, they called out to the guards to help them climb out of the six-foot-deep hole they had dug. Laughing, the guards threw the dead woman's body on top of Zisi and then began shovelling fresh mud back into the grave on top of the terrified women. Zisi and her two friends screamed and begged for help. The only way out was to step on the body of Zisi's cousin and receive a helping hand from the smirking guards. When all three had managed to climb to safety, they collapsed exhausted on the ground, still with the feeling of the flesh of Libshe's body under their feet.

In the days following this incident, Zisi became ill. She was covered in blisters and red spots, her body ached and she was exhausted. For several days, she lay in bed and was unable to work. Malchi became very concerned as Zisi's optimism and strength began to falter. Then an opportunity came along. One morning, one of the guards announced that a shoemaker was needed. With Yaakov – Chaya's father – in mind, Zisi volunteered, telling the guard that her father was a shoemaker.

She drew on the hours of watching Chaya's father working at his trade, in the hope that it might save her from having to return to the munitions factory. The first pair of shoes that she made were a complete disaster, uncomfortable, with no distinction between left and right. The other shoemakers and prisoners tried to cover up for her but couldn't prevent her from being beaten for such bad work. Nevertheless, she soon learnt the trade and, no longer being forced to march to work every day at the munitions factory with its noxious fumes, found herself able to rebuild her strength. In addition, she and Malchi were able to work occasionally on a small vegetable garden and provide their friends with carrots and other fresh food.

At night, the women in Zisi's barrack, lying exhausted in bed, would continually talk of freedom, speculating on what they would do if and when they got out of captivity. Much of the conversation would focus on food. They would compare recipes and argue over the best way to cook chicken soup or cheesecake.

One thing they all agreed upon was that when they were free they would always carry a loaf of bread with them. Zisi often dreamt of a fresh, hot loaf – no butter, no jam, just bread. This was luxury enough. She could often hear the woman in the bunk below hers sighing longingly as she looked up at the photo of a loaf of bread that she had stuck to the bottom of Zisi's bunk.

15

At an agreed signal, nine or ten women, including Zisi and Malchi, ran for the trees

One day in late January 1945, six months after Zisi had been taken into Brannau, some of her comrades returned from their shift in a state of high excitement. The munitions factory had been alive with rumours of the Russian advance upon the German lines. They were already nearby, it was said, and were advancing daily.

While the camp guards were becoming increasingly nervous, the inmates experienced hope for the first time. But nobody really knew what to expect; the guards were on edge and the women prisoners began to prepare themselves for the worst. Fearing an attack by the guards, Zisi advised everyone to gather up sharp objects with a view to their being used in self-defence. A plan to cut the telephone lines to prevent massacre orders from getting through was also devised.

In the event, these emergency measures were never put into action. The inmates were caught completely by surprise one freezing morning when guards burst in and ordered them to be ready to leave in thirty minutes. But, once outside, the women were made to stand for several hours in the bitter cold. Snow lay on the ground when Zisi and Malchi were placed together in one of the endless ranks of five. Alongside them were Zisi's friend Irene, from Mukačevo and Irene's mother.

When, finally, the order was given to march, Irene's mother strode ahead as if she was in the usual situation of being urged on by the guards' cries of "*Schnell Schnell!*". But other prisoners quietly warned: "Slow down, slow down, the Russians are not far away. Take it as slowly as possible."

The march continued north-east towards the Baltic with only short breaks and without any food or water being distributed. During the breaks, the women relieved themselves and ate handfuls of snow. By the evening, frozen and exhausted, they were herded into a barn, where they could cover themselves with hay and try to rest. Sleep proved impossible. It was a deeply cold night; the wind blew continually through gaps in the barn's roof and walls; and the air was filled with the groaning of prisoners who were in pain from the relentless marching. For Zisi her only source of strength was to close her eyes and to focus on her twinkling star.

At first light, the familiar cry, "*Heraus, Heraus!*", brought the women to their feet and out of the barn for a roll-call. When the numbers did not add up, the German officers went into the barn, loudly screaming for those hiding in the hay to show themselves. But this was not enough and the guards set fire to the barn to smoke out anyone hiding. Then, with flames burning and smoke billowing out into the dawn air, they ordered everyone into position and set off once more.

The snow had deepened overnight and the march became more and more hazardous as the unfortunate prisoners, with the SS guards yelling at them, had to wade through knee-deep snow to keep up. During one of the brief breaks, Zisi sat down to relieve her cold and weary feet. She felt her head spin but, despite the icy cold that was slowly spreading through her body, she decided to stay where she was and not move any more. In her desperate mental state, she longed simply to let go so that she would no longer feel the cold or have to drag her feet beneath her. Malchi and Irene saw that Zisi was slowly sinking and pulled her to her feet. They shook her as vigorously as they could and forced her to keep moving. But, with their strength declining and the march seemingly never-ending, Zisi, Malchi and a handful of others decided that, rather than go along with their German captors in their desperate drive to evade the pursuing Red Army, they would take the first opportunity to escape.

Some time later, they found themselves approaching a small forest. As they drew alongside it, at an agreed signal, nine or ten women, including Zisi and Malchi, ran for the trees. Their escape did not go unnoticed but, in defiance of the orders to halt and the warning cries, they continued running, with a couple of guards in pursuit. The guards' shouting became louder as they drew nearer, the fleeing women dispersed into small groups and four of them slipped behind a wall in the corner of a small, two-storey building. Crouching low, they waited in complete silence, holding their breath. They could hear the guards' voices, one male and one female, and their footsteps on the gravel getting louder. The desperate prisoners reacted by squeezing themselves together in as small a huddle as they could manage, trying to make themselves invisible. Expecting to be blinded by torchlight at any moment, they could hardly believe it when the heavy boots and voices passed them by and faded into the distance. The group remained huddled together for some time until they felt it safe to continue.

Relief then turned immediately to terror as none of them was able to move. They were all frozen to the ground.

Though crying and shivering from fear, they wriggled and worked themselves free until they all managed to stand and continue their journey into the woods. The further they penetrated, the darker it became, but they could not stop for fear of freezing to death.

By now, the Russian army was within earshot and every so often its men were sending flares – known as "Stalin lights" – into the night sky. Zisi and her comrades told themselves the beams were informing them that the Russians knew they were there and wanted to guide them to safety. The intermittent illumination created by the Stalin lights revealed a group of small houses at the edge of the woods. Unable to continue and desperate for warmth and food, the escapers decided to risk discovery by asking for help. Fearful of confronting Nazis, however, they avoided knocking on the first, second and third doors and only at the fourth house did they decide to approach and knock. Receiving no answer, they simply pushed the door open and walked in.

16

They took off their clothes in order to pick out and crush the lice

Once inside the house, the four friends could hardly believe their eyes. Although nobody was present, a fire was burning in the grate and a table was laid with food. The residents must have only recently departed, in fear of the approach of the Russians. The starving young Jewish women sat down and ate as they had not done in months, and then fell asleep in warmth and comfort, no longer caring who might find them.

The next morning, their bodies paid dearly for their feast of the previous evening with stomach cramps, diarrhoea and sickness. They were too weak to move and so, when no one came to claim the house, Zisi and her friends stayed where they were to recuperate. They took it in turns to keep watch.

After several days the girl keeping watch rushed in one morning to warn the others that a German soldier was nearing the house. Locking the doors and, as best they could, hiding any signs of life, they kept silent until he had passed. Later, a Russian soldier came by and stopped to help them. Pointing at the numbers still sewn on their sleeves, he said they were no longer necessary and cut them off. He fixed the frozen pump outside the house to enable them to obtain fresh water and he gathered wood for the fire. After this lone Russian soldier, many more Russian soldiers passed by in numbers, many of them warning that a group of women alone would not be safe and that the girls should move on to a refugee centre that had been set up nearby.

After two weeks in the comfort of this house, food was in very short supply and the girls were already showing the signs of poor nutrition and lack of vegetables. They tried to find the cellar where vegetables and potatoes were kept but were unable to find the entrance. Driven by hunger, they captured a young calf. None of them had any idea of how to slaughter an animal and, in desperation, they began to throw stones at the bemused creature, whose pleading eyes soon caused them to stop.

Eventually, some more Russian soldiers came by, sent the women away, and killed the animal for them. When it came to it, however, Zisi and her comrades found themselves unable to eat it. The lack of food and their anxiety that some of the increasing numbers of Russian army personnel passing by might take advantage of such a helpless band of young women, prompted them to seek out the refugee centre about which they had been told.

When they found it, they were greeted warmly and given something to eat and coffee to drink. Nevertheless, for all the supply of adequate food and in spite of the sense of safety in numbers, the night was constantly disturbed by frightened collaborators offering food and shelter in exchange for promises of protection from the Russians. One after another, local people came to Zisi and her friends pleading: "Remember my name – tell the soldiers that I helped you." In view of this and the lack of sleep and the overcrowding, Zisi and Malchi decided it was time to start their journey home.

It was March 1945, five weeks since they had left Brannau. Zisi and Malchi left the company of Irene, her mother and other escapees to start their journey home. As they made their way south towards the Polish border they met scores of other Jewish refugees and exchanged news of friends and family, advice as to how to travel and other pieces of useful information. "Be careful of the soldiers," they were told, "stay in busy places". Constantly harassed by triumphant, drunken Russian soldiers in search of *barishnias* (women) and hearing terrible stories of rape, Zisi, Malchi and new friends found en route sought refuge in the most unlikely places. Occasionally, in the extreme cold of the night they would accept the hospitality of local people trying to protect themselves from the wrath of the Russians.

The young escapees joined the great mass of people slowly progressing towards the southern Polish border. With no money, food or map, they were utterly dependent on the goodwill of others to guide them in the right direction and to provide them with scraps of food. At night, they encountered other refugees, prisoners of war and escaping soldiers occupying private houses and, with no alternative, stopped for the night in fear, not knowing whom they could trust.

Poland at the end of the war was mayhem. The country was teeming with thousands of refugees; freed prisoners of war; displaced Poles searching for their homes and families, Nazi collaborators on the run from the Russians and thousands of celebrating Russian soldiers making their presence felt in every town and village. Houses abandoned by collaborators were openly available for those in transit. Trains were packed.

Zisi and Malchi made their way slowly through devastated towns and cities. Hearing that Warsaw was in ruins and filled with refugees, they decided to go instead to Lodz. On arrival, they were shocked by the devastation.

A once-beautiful city had been completely flattened. They could not find shelter in the city itself and sought and found it briefly on the outskirts, before moving on.

After leaving Lodz, a group of nervous Latvian soldiers joined them, offering to protect them from the advances of Russian soldiers. The Latvians had changed their uniforms for civilian clothes and walked together with Zisi and Malchi.

The Latvians' protection proved effective, since the Russian soldiers were less likely to harass the girls when they were accompanied by other men – and less likely to suspect men accompanied by refugees. On one occasion, when they had stopped for a rest, the Latvian soldiers gave the Jewish girls their boots and advised Zisi and Malchi to hide under a blanket next to them. When Russian soldiers came looking for *barishnias*, all they saw were men's boots sticking out from under the blanket. Disappointed, they turned away.

No longer with their Latvian protectors, the sisters' long, harsh journey continued. At each place they stopped they met other groups of refugees similarly making their way home. They rarely stayed with the same people for more than a few days as each had their own agenda and their own route to follow. Weak and hungry, lacking water and proper sanitary conditions, Zisi and Malchi continued to make their way through areas of devastation. They suffered from blisters, sores and stomach problems and were plagued all over their bodies by lice. On one occasion, they took off their clothes in order to pick out and crush the lice, managing to find replacement warm clothing along the way. They were so exhausted from the lack of food, the journey and the harassment from the Russian soldiers that when Zisi and Malchi found a place to stay where they felt safe, they were inclined to remain there for several days. However, such was their burning wish to reach their home and see their father, that they continued to the Polish border with Soviet-occupied, Subcarpathian Rus'.

As they got closer to the border, Zisi and Malchi learned that their home town had changed hands once more. In August 1944 the Soviet Army had reached the Carpathian mountains and by the end of October they controlled all of Subcarpathian Rus'. With the Hungarians and Germans removed from the area and with no intention of returning the area to Czechoslovakia, the Russians were planning to incorporate it into the USSR.

17

*Day after day she would wake seeing the images of these children
and force herself to go out and continue the waiting, searching
and questioning*

Zisi and Malchi were kept going throughout their gruelling trek across Poland by their determination to get home, where they always believed they would meet their father waiting for them. It was June 1945 as they neared the border with their now Soviet-occupied homeland, when Zisi met her friend, Shifra, from Mukačevo, who had been at the brick factory waiting for a train with her. So overjoyed was she to see Shifra, she took it as a hopeful sign that she would find other friends back home in Mukačevo.

There were many other Jewish refugees gathered near the border and, like Zisi and Malchi, all were desperate to get back home to see their families and put their recent horrific experiences behind them. Among these many physically and mentally scarred individuals was a large number of Polish Jews who, on returning to their devastated homes had been greeted with the same terrible anti-Semitism that they had encountered before and during the war. These refugees had no wish to rebuild their lives in Poland and were therefore tempted by the Russian promise of equality and freedom. But it was not always easy for these Jews to cross the border, because the Polish authorities endeavoured to stop them from leaving. Having befriended some of the Polish Jews who were stranded and frustrated at the border, Zisi made the first of several important decisions.

By scattering a few Poles in among groups of Hungarian and Czech refugees, Zisi, Shifra and other friends were able to walk back and forth across the border on several occasions without the Poles being detected. After a week, the pull of home was too strong and she decided to move on and follow Malchi to Mukačevo. She and Shifra left together and boarded the train to Mukačevo.

As their train drew into Mukačevo, the station was teeming with people. Looking through the window, Zisi recognised many of the anxious faces behind placards bearing the names of missing family members. As she and Shifra left the railway station, people called to her, asking for news of their loved ones, and old friends and neighbours reached out to shake her hand or embrace her. As well as being asked for information, she was also given some. "Your brother Moishe is alive – he is living in the home of a gypsy woman," one person told her. Another confirmed that: "Malchi returned a few days ago – she is very worried about you."

Zisi, accompanied by Shifra, headed straight for Bereksaz. By the time she reached the corner of her street, she was in a state of great excitement and expectancy. In her mind's eye, she pictured her father studying at the table where he always had done. She even recalled the sight of her late mother standing on the courtyard steps and the house itself looking resplendent in the sunshine. But, as the house came into view, these visions turned into a nightmare.

The Düm family home was now a shell, without doors, windows, furniture or carpets. Rain had come through holes in the roof; floorboards had been pulled up and, as Zisi passed through the house, her footsteps echoed through hollow, empty rooms. So overcome with emotion was she, tears falling and her head spinning, that she collapsed on to the floor and Shifra had to help her to sit against the wall. When she managed to get up, she saw through the window that the courtyard appeared to be covered with a thin, white coating of snow – in May! Then, as she looked more closely, she gasped as she recognised thousands of fragments of pages from her father's books, strewn across the ground.

Unable to stay in the house a moment longer, Zisi hurried out with Shifra into the street. Completely dazed and wondering how she was going to find Malchi, she was approached by a neighbour who invited her and Shifra into her home for a coffee. As she sat in this friendly woman's house, Zisi immediately spotted one of her own family's carpets. The woman reddened visibly but said nothing and Zisi and Shifra left as soon as possible.

Back out on the street, Zisi entered the courtyard and crossed it to enter the cellar. The hole in the ground where she and Malchi had hidden their mother's jewellery was empty but embedded in the cracks by the window were the gold coins that Zisi had hidden as a diversion. She took these and rejoined Shifra on the street. She walked away without looking back. She knew that she would never see the house again.

By this time, word had got around that Zisi had returned. She was approached by other refugees who told her where to find Malchi and her brother Moishe. Now recovered from the initial shock of seeing the destroyed and looted building that once had been the family home, Zisi parted company with Shifra, promising to visit her soon, and followed the directions she had been given to a gypsy woman's home on the edge of town. Here, she was finally reunited with her brother Moishe and a very worried Malchi, who still had no news of Shimi.

After an emotional reunion with Malchi and Moishe, she was greeted by their benefactor, a beautiful and kind gypsy woman, named Viola. Viola advised Zisi to go outside and remove her clothes in order to wash them – and herself – thoroughly to get rid of the lice. As a gypsy, Viola had also suffered at the hands of the Nazis and had offered her home to many Jewish refugees. Her boyfriend, a Russian Jewish soldier, would often bring meat and other good things for everyone to eat, warning the occupying soldiers to take good care of Viola and all who stayed with her.

In this uncomfortable but secure environment, Zisi, Malchi and Moishe enjoyed other's company while hoping that they would soon be reunited with other family members. While waiting for his sisters to arrive, Moishe had approached Solentoyneni, the woman who had run the family shop in their name, and she had agreed to give them some of the money left with her following their departure, plus some rolls of fabric to help them maintain their income. This money and the gold coins that Zisi had retrieved from the cellar allowed them to get by and pay Viola for her hospitality.

After several days' recuperation and with no further word from any other family members, Zisi was anxious to at least find some of her old friends. Several family friends had already come to see them at Viola's home but Zisi wanted to find out about her own friends. Together with Shifra, she spent a lot of time meeting and talking to other Jews in town and was slowly able to piece together what had happened to many of her friends. There were several stories similar to hers and accounts of terrible loss, but few talked about their own personal stories, finding it easier to talk about others.

For every happy reunion, there were several tragic stories. She met Yenti from Bereksaz, from whom she learned that Mogda would not return. Meeting her old friend Moishe from Hashomer Hatzair and his sister Rivka, she heard of the terrible fate of their younger sister and their parents and were still awaiting news of their older sister Shoshi. Tears were shed over and over again as friends recounted the last time they had seen their parents, their children, their nephews and nieces.

The more of these appalling, sad stories Zisi heard, the more they confirmed her deepest fears that her dear father would never return and that she would never see the sweet faces of Juditko and Hava, never again experience the warm touch of Fishi.

Her heart ached to think that she might never know what had happened to Eti, her Achi, and her children, who had disappeared in 1942; her brother Shloime and his wife Surchu, with whom she had spent so much time; Gizi and her children; Ruchtu and Ushi, or her sister Sari and her baby daughter.

Day after day, she would wake seeing the images of these children and force herself to go out and continue the waiting, the searching and the questioning of the constant stream of refugees arriving home to Mukačevo.

18

They would need to understand that the journey would be hard and there was no guarantee that they would get into Palestine

After a couple of weeks, with still no news of other family members, Moishe, Malchi and Zisi thanked Viola for her kindness and found a temporary home in an abandoned apartment. The additional space and comfort of these new surroundings, and the visits there by more and more old friends, sadly were scant compensation for the helplessness the three siblings felt while waiting, with diminishing hope, for news of other members of their family.

Finally, in early July when she returned from visiting friends, Zisi's patience was rewarded with news that her sister Sari was on her way to Mukačevo. News had reached Sari in Kosice that some of her family were alive and so she made the four-hour journey to Mukačevo, where she was directed to the apartment and a poignant reunion with her brother and two sisters. The mood was not entirely celebratory, for Sari had a painful story to tell.

Sari described how she and her husband Erno, having left Mukačevo in 1942 for Kosice, had managed to continue working in the family business with Erno's brothers until 1944, when they bought false papers with Christian identities, enabling them to leave Kosice. By that time, Miryam Rivka, their daughter, was just under a year old. Knowing that they had every chance of being caught, they decided to bribe a local doctor to keep Miryam in the hospital in his safekeeping. Sari and Erno left Erno's family and travelled at night with their false papers to Budapest. They successfully passed themselves off as Christians and pretended that Erno had been sent to Budapest to manage a factory. Once in the Hungarian capital, they rented a room from the widow of a government minister. Sari befriended the woman and Erno went off to "work" every day, in reality spending most of his time hiding in the waiting rooms of various dentists across town.

In this fashion, they managed to survive. At the end of the war, they returned to Kosice and contacted the doctor into whose safekeeping they had given their daughter. At this point in her narrative, Sari broke down. With difficulty, she explained that the doctor, with great sadness, had told her that baby Miryam had been taken away by the Nazis. Unable to believe him and suspecting that he might have taken Miryam Rivka to raise her as his own daughter, Sari and Erno returned a number of times to the doctor and pleaded for their child's return. But they always returned empty-handed.

Sari did not want to leave her brother and sisters again and urged them to leave Mukačevo and return with her to Kosice where she and Erno had a big enough apartment and where they would be able to find work. After a few days deliberation, they agreed. By this time, they'd had word that both Ruchtu and Shimi were still alive and on their way to Mukačevo and, having agreed to Sari's suggestion, they left messages with their friends to tell any returning family members how to contact them in Kosice. It ought to have been a wrench to leave Mukačevo but they all experienced a great sense of relief at leaving their home town, tarnished as it now was with shattered dreams and bad memories.

Erno's father had owned a textile business in Kosice and, with what was left of the business, Erno and his brothers resumed trading. Having received some rolls of fabric from the Düm family store in Mukačevo, Moishe also managed to find a ready market. He, Malchi and Zisi would take it in turns to travel out of Kosice in order to bring back cigarettes and textiles, which were in short supply.

After just a few days in Kosice, they were finally reunited with Ruchtu, who, having gone first to Satmar, then Mukačevo, went on to Kosice. Zisi had waited to meet Ruchtu again with some trepidation. On their last meeting, Ruchtu had left Fishi with Zisi and travelled with her son Ushi back to Satmar. With no word from Fishi, Zisi desperately hoped that Ushi had survived. But it was not to be. Ruchtu had simultaneously been hoping that Fishi had managed to stay with Zisi and Malchi. Once again, the joy and relief at seeing a sister alive could only be partial. In this case, it was overwhelmed by grief at Ruchtu's loss of her husband and both of her sons, Ushi and Fishi.

As the brothers and sisters struggled with their new reality, they attempted to explore opportunities in areas of the world less affected by the war. Erno discussed making contact with cousins in Australia. Zisi's brother Fishel wrote from America urging them to come and join him there. Ruchtu got in touch with their uncle Heskel in Belgium. But no one talked openly about the future. Having just found each other again, each one of them felt compelled to stay with the others and wait for any further news of surviving family members.

Every morning, Zisi would force herself to rise from bed and join her sisters in preparing food for the rest of the family. Sometimes, she would accompany Moishe on a trip to buy merchandise for sale or to Mukačevo to get money from Matush who had taken over the management of her sister Gizi's fur shop. Matush was a Communist and deeply sympathetic towards the Düm family. He had kept their money on deposit and arranged with them to come to see him on a monthly basis when he would withdraw money for them.

But it was becoming increasingly hard for Zisi to drag herself out of bed in the morning. When she awoke she would automatically look for her father or her mother, or for Fishi and the other nieces and nephews. And when she went to Mukačevo or was out in Kosice, she would find herself searching for familiar faces – for the children she knew had gone. The stark reality was that there were no children left for her to find. No sounds of youthful laughter, or street games; no affectionate calling by mothers to their children to come home and get ready for dinner.

And that was not all. Even in the hastily set-up Jewish section of the market in Mukačevo, she could recognise no familiar faces. There were no older people to help across the street, no wise relatives to go to for advice, no rabbis or community elders to bring the Jewish community together again. Slowly, she came to realise that the only Jewish faces that she would ever see in both Kosice and Mukačevo would be those of young women and men like herself, strong enough to have survived slave labour and worse. It was time to move on.

It was during this period of adjustment that Malchi's long vigil came to an end. Having heard from several people that Shimi was alive and making his way to Mukačevo, she couldn't wait to welcome him back. When he did arrive, in early August 1945, he too had quite a story to tell. Having spent the duration of the war as a prisoner in Russia, he had been made to walk across vast areas of that country as a human bomb detector, before being recaptured by the Germans, who incarcerated him in Mauthausen concentration camp, where he stayed until the end of the war.

Perhaps Shimi's return was what Zisi needed to spur her into action. It would have been almost unimaginable for her to leave Malchi again if Shimi had not returned. But when he did, Zisi began to allow herself to think about her future. With Russia now in formal control of the area following the Czech-Soviet treaty of June 1945, there were rumours that the Soviets planned to close their borders and so the family members started to make plans. With Erno being encouraged to come to Australia, Moishe investigating ways to get a visa to enter the US to be with his brother Fishel and Ruchtu in contact with her uncle in Belgium, Zisi's mind turned to Palestine.

During her journey through Poland, many people she met had talked of groups travelling to Palestine. On returning to Mukačevo, many of her friends mentioned Jewish groups helping people make their way across Europe to Palestine. During the war, it turned out, the Hashomer and Hechalutz youth movements had remained active and were now very busy training would-be immigrants for collective life on *kibbutzim* in Palestine. Other organisations were busy negotiating passage for Jewish refugees into Palestine, and yet more were busy arranging places for these refugees to stay while making the long journey to Palestine.

At the forefront of all this effort was the American Jewish Joint Distribution Committee – better known as "the Joint". Established in 1918 to provide relief to Jews around the world, in the post-Second World war period the Joint focused its efforts on rehabilitation and training of refugees to prepare them for a new life in Palestine.

Zisi's determination to find her way to Palestine was strengthened by hearing about these initiatives. But there was one major hurdle to get over. How could she leave her brothers and sisters with little certainty of when she would see them again? How could she say goodbye to Malchi, Moishe and Sari after having only recently been reunited with them? She knew that if she told them about her plans they would do everything to stop her. She also knew that she would not be able to say goodbye to them face to face.

In late September 1945, four months after her return, Zisi found her opportunity. She decided to accompany Shimi on a business trip that included Mukačevo, with a view to seeking friends' assistance to prepare for the journey to Palestine. Like her, they would need to understand that the journey would be hard and there was no guarantee that they would get into the country. Zisi's own response to these potential drawbacks was to reaffirm her determination to try, whatever the obstacles. She could no longer sit and wait for people who would never return, no longer live amid the remains of her previous, destroyed existence, or without the sound of young children and older people around her.

She and Shimi rose early for the fateful trip and, before they set out, Zisi left a letter for her family telling them that she would be in touch but that she was not coming back. On arrival in Mukačevo, she parted company with Shimi, telling him she would meet him again in Kosice.

She busied herself making contact with friends, hoping to find someone with whom to share the journey. She learned that assistance for those wishing to go to Palestine was available in Bucharest, where Hashomer Hatzair was organising groups of young people to travel. And Bucharest, Zisi discovered from Chaya's sister Rachel, was where Chaya was at that moment. She was, though, very sick and Rachel was preparing to travel to join her in

Bucharest. Shifra, with whom Zisi had returned from Poland, had already left Mukačevo for Palestine.

But Zisi did find a willing companion in her old friend Moishe. His sister Rivka had already left for Palestine and upon hearing that his older sister Shoshi had also survived and was already in Palestine, he was intent on travelling there to be reunited with them. Moishe and Zisi agreed to leave for Bucharest together. Zisi paid one last visit to Solentoyneni in order to get some money for her journey and, that night, she and Moishe boarded a train out of Mukačevo.

Mukačevo was now occupied by Russia and crossing the borders required special permits that the two travellers did not possess. Two days and two trains later, Zisi and Moishe found themselves climbing to the top of a mountain of coal in a coal truck on a train heading for Bucharest, which is how they crossed the Romanian border. Once they had done so, they found many other young Jews concealed in the same train, all travelling to Bucharest with the same intention.

19

"What is Kaddish?", the Russian officer asked

When Zisi and Moishe arrived at the Hashomer Hatzair offices in Bucharest, they were thrilled to learn how well-organised things were. With funding from international bodies such as the Joint, Hashomer was able to supply maps, guides and provisions for the journey to Palestine. Its staff also invested a great deal of time in preparing the migrants for their new life. There were courses in nursing, teaching, farming and agriculture, including specialist farming skills that were needed to drain the swamps, grow crops and build new communities. The buzz of purposeful activity and the determination of the young people around her lifted Zisi's spirits.

She and Moishe were both allocated Jewish families to stay with during this time and different departure dates for Palestine. So, saying farewell to Moishe, she and another woman were sent to a Jewish family called Rosen, who immediately accepted them into their modest home. During the war, Bucharest had been a haven for Jews, where they were protected by the Rumanian Government. Here, in contrast to her last days in Mukačevo, there was an abundance of both young and old people. Zisi experienced a sense of restored normality.

After about ten days Zisi was allocated to a Hashomer group of approximately 20 people to travel to Italy, where they would wait for a boat to Palestine. The route was planned for them, with contacts to link up with at various points and travel documents and train tickets arranged. They set off on a train from Bucharest to Budapest, where they were once again greeted by members of Hashomer Hatzair, who issued them with further documents and instructions during a four-day stopover. Zisi took advantage of this to find her Uncle Heskel, who had survived with his family by digging a cellar under their house and hiding there throughout 1944. When discovered by the Germans, he and his family were deported to Budapest for transportation to the camps.

While waiting for the trains to take them away, Budapest was surrounded by Russian troops and so they remained in Budapest and avoided the concentration camps. Heskel and his wife, Fiege received their niece warmly and tried to convince her to stay longer with them but Zisi was determined to continue her journey, the next stage of which was a train ride to Graz, in Austria.

In Graz, the young migrant group were put up in a small hotel where, for twenty-four hours, Zisi and the others were taught German phrases, to help authenticate their claim that they were Austrians returning to their homes in the British-controlled zone of the country. Late the next evening, they gathered together to be given their final instructions. They were to walk quietly in twos through a hilly, woodland area until they were almost at the border with the British Zone, where they would meet representatives of the Jewish Brigade, who would lead them across the boundary. The Brigade had been set up by the British in Palestine in 1944, where Jewish soldiers served as part of the British Army's efforts in Italy. After the war these same soldiers turned their efforts to helping fellow Jews make their way across Europe and enter Palestine.

Zisi found the directions so confusing that she decided to rely on others to lead the way. But then she found herself walking alongside an old friend from Mukačevo whom she had not seen since before the establishment of the ghetto. The pair literally got lost in conversation and suddenly found themselves not knowing which way to go. The people behind had been relying on them to keep track of the leaders and were furious when they found they were lost. Trying to remember the instructions, they continued walking, only to find themselves face-to-face with a group of Russian soldiers. Not wanting to be forced to return to Mukačevo, the Hashomer members took great care not to show any understanding of Russian. Speaking German as directed, they claimed to be Austrians returning to the British Zone. This, however, turned out to be a dangerous move. The Russian soldiers suspected that they were Nazis or collaborators in hiding and marched them off through the town. The local populace, eager to demonstrate their newly discovered hatred for the Nazis, jumped to the same conclusion and started throwing stones and spitting at the Hashomer members, who spent that night locked in a small room.

In the morning, they were brought before a young Russian officer. Once again, they were asked who they were and where they were going. Fearful of telling him they were Jews, they tried to maintain their original story in German. The officer then suddenly stopped and asked them rather different questions.

"What is Kaddish?" he asked and followed up with a series of other

Hebrew words and customs, which he asked them to translate and explain. Wondering whether this officer was himself Jewish, they tentatively began to give proper answers to his questions. When he smiled in response, the Hashomer group relaxed and told him the truth – that they were on their way to Palestine.

The officer immediately offered to help. He ordered his men to escort the anxious migrants to a house in the town. Here, while the Jewish officer made arrangements for their safe passage, they were able to freshen up and unwind and even, in some cases, visit the hairdresser with the little money they had. Three days later, the officer instructed his soldiers to guide them safely to a village near the border. From there, following the officer's directions, they would walk to the border, where the Jewish Brigade would be expecting them.

When they reached the border, Brigade members were waiting, just as promised. Each person received a food parcel and drink as they climbed on to a waiting truck. As Zisi was clambering aboard, a voice called out: "Zisi, come and sit with me." She turned to see the smiling face of the truck driver – an old schoolfriend from Mukačevo. He repeated his invitation and she went to sit with him at the front of the truck and they chatted throughout the journey across the Austrian and Italian Alps towards Modena.

From her privileged seat, Zisi had a wonderful view of the surrounding area. After 14 hours punctuated with brief stops, they finally arrived in Modena, where they were taken to a large transit camp containing hundreds of refugees. Food was plentiful and the atmosphere optimistic among the excited young arrivals, happy to be on the last leg of their journey to Palestine. Over the next few days, they were free to explore the town, whose opera house became a huge attraction. Every night, 20 free tickets were given to refugees. Zisi had never seen an opera before and was enthralled.

Nevertheless, despite the security of the camp and the friendly nature of the locals, Zisi and her friends grew restless when it became clear that they would be kept for an indefinite period in the overcrowded conditions. When some of the Hashomer Hatzair members searched for somewhere else to stay, they were told by fellow members about a house by the sea near Rome where they would be able to stay until a boat could be found willing to take them "illegally" to Palestine.

Leaving the transit camp was not easy; having registered, they were expected to return every evening. But the rebellious group, including Zisi, went ahead with their plans, leaving with small bags at various times during the day. Once they were all gathered, Zisi found herself travelling together with 20 other young people, most of them somewhat different from her. The majority were Lithuanian and Romanian partisans who spoke a strain of Yiddish that Zisi could not understand. Travelling through the night, Zisi felt uncomfortable and out of place. She regretted having left the refugee camp, where there were many people from her background.

Early the next morning, the group arrived in Rome to be taken to a small hotel. Despite their exhaustion, they were all excited to be in Rome and so they immediately left the hotel to explore. As they were leaving, they looked up at the sign in order to remember the name of their hotel and memorised the word: "Albergo". When it grew dark and they were tired and hungry, they started to make their way back. To their surprise, they soon discovered several hotels with the "Albergo" sign and it dawned on them that *albergo* was Italian for hotel! They wandered the streets for several hours until somone stopped to help them. Recognising that they were refugees, he guessed which hotel might have taken them.

After this adventure with the group, Zisi shed her misgivings about having left the refugee camp. By the end of their week in Rome, she regarded them as family and was happy to spend the next few months with them, waiting for a boat to Palestine.

20

*During daylight, the passengers were required to remain below deck
so as not to be spotted*

From Rome, the now tightly knit band of refugees were taken to the nearby seaside resort of Ostia and installed in an unfurnished villa. Every day, Zisi would shake out her blouse and skirt, the only clothing she possessed, and spend the day sitting and walking on the beach, swimming with her house-mates, or meeting other young Jews living nearby who were also waiting to depart for Palestine. From here, after many months of silence, she finally wrote to her sisters and brothers in Kosice, telling them that she was safe in Italy. She hoped that her letter would still find them.

The splendid setting and the freedom they enjoyed were ample compensation for the scarcity of food. Every day, the soldiers from the Jewish Brigade would bring food supplies sent by the Joint (American Jewish Joint Distribution Committee) – or taken from British army stores. After a couple of weeks, the soldiers brought them sewing machines, sheets and other fabrics so that they could work and earn some money. This helped alleviate the food shortage, although that was something that hardly bothered Zisi, so enchanted was she by the sea. She spent hour upon hour swimming and sunbathing. The rest of the time, when she was not working at the sewing machine, she would attend lectures run by Hashomer Hatzair, followed by community singing around a fire. For Zisi, this was a wonderful time, of first romance with a young Rumanian called Nelu Kovalu, close friendships, freedom and a nourishing of the soul.

Winter came and these twenty young people were still waiting, comfortably ensconced in Ostia. In addition to her friendship with Nelu, she became particularly close to a woman called Chana Blonder. She also met up frequently with Rivka, the sister of Moishe (her friend from Mukačevo) who was living in a nearby house, also on her way to Palestine. To keep the house warm, the house-mates collected wood and pine-cones from the nearby forest, although venturing outside was itself uncomfortable, as they had scarcely any warm clothing.

After three months in Ostia, towards the end of February, they were told that the time had come to move on. For fear that conversation might spread outside the group, they were not told where they were going until they were safely aboard a bus that took them to Genoa in the middle of the night.

On the bus, they were split into two groups. A pair of sisters were initially separated, creating confusion, protest and tears. Having been together through so much, the sisters were demonstrating loudly and forcefully against their separation. Desperate not to miss the boat, a few passengers created a distraction by singing: "*Es Brent Yiddelach es Brent,* " – "It's burning, little Jews, it's burning."

Zisi waited nervously until the sisters were reunited and she was able to concentrate on the instructions to the group in which she had been placed. They were to make their way quietly, without being seen or heard, to the Enso Sereni, a ship named after the Italian Zionist of the same name.

The bus arrived at Genoa dock and Zisi and her friends walked quickly and silently to the Enso Sereni. The lower deck of the boat was crammed with people, young and old, parents and children, sitting squeezed along the sides. Once aboard, Zisi peered round the door of one of the cabins and was met with a similar sight of families squashed together on bunks. She and Chana Blonder managed to find a free bunk on which to squash up together and prepare themselves for a long, crowded journey on a choppy, wintry sea.

During daylight, the passengers were required to remain below deck so as not to be spotted. With the boat flying a Turkish flag and its human cargo out of sight, it was hoped that suspicions would not be aroused on British aircraft and ships. At night, passengers were allowed to go out on deck to breathe fresh, sea air and escape from the stench below.

After several days at sea, they were hit by a severe storm. The passengers had to use their body weight to balance the boat, get rid of excess water and prevent the deck becoming flooded. In spite of these difficult conditions, Zisi retained an overwhelming optimism. She felt almost invincible. When the ship stopped suddenly at sea, fear never entered her mind. Instead, she and her friends laughingly described how they would swim to Palestine if necessary.

Food was carefully rationed among the passengers. The small pieces of chocolate, few sips of water, some soup and bread were barely enough, but no one complained. On particularly rough days, many people were too sick to eat. Luckily, the rough seas did not affect Zisi and so she benefited from finishing off others' neglected portions of soup.

After a fortnight, the sound of planes overhead alerted them to possible British suspicions – they were nearing their destination. From this point on, they were even more careful to stay below deck – but not Zisi. Curious as ever, when she heard the aircraft engines overhead, she crept out and found a place to hide herself out on the deck. It was pitch black and, as the sound of the planes subsided, the ship started to gather speed. The crew explained to her that they were going to try to make it to land at night, when they might not be seen. Pointing to the shoreline, they told her to look out for the lights of the bay of Haifa.

Straining her eyes to see, a familiar vision came to her – the little star that she had been able to conjure up in the past, at times when she needed strength, by closing her eyes. The star that she had so often seen when she was at her lowest, her Glimmer of Hope. This time, though, her eyes were wide open and the star was now a guiding light directly in front of her.

"Somehow," Zisi was later to recall, "I knew I had arrived. I was home."

From left to right:
Rav David Schlussel
with his wife Sara
(left) and his son
Heskel Schlussel
with his wife Feige

Above: Malchi with son
Moishe and Naomi with
son Jonathan 1957

Left: Naomi with Malchi
1952

Opposite: Naomi's mother

The sisters at the wedding
of Malchi's daughter Ada
1965. From left to right:
Naomi, Sari, Ada, Malchi,
Ruchtu

Opposite, top: Malchi
and Shimi in Madrid with
children 1953

Opposite, below: Sari and
Erno with their son George
1950

Opposite, bottom: Sister
Ruchtu with Heskel
Schlussel and his son 1950

Above, top: Naomi with
brother Moishe 1985

Above: brother Moishe with
wife Rosa 1985

Opposite, top: Naomi,
Malchi, Shimi and grandson
Moishe

Opposite, below: sister Sari
with her sons, Tomy (left)
and George (right)

View of Mukačevo
(Mukacheve) 1994

NAOMI'S STORY

21

The bedraggled bunch of arrivals cried out in horror as they were
asked to strip, shower and go through the delousing process

Although Zisi might have reached the home stretch, she was not yet "home". Just before sunrise, a few hours after that first, nocturnal glimpse of the bay of Haifa, she and the other passengers were awoken by a voice on a loud speaker. A warning came from the deck that a British boat was approaching. This was a signal to any men on board who were carrying guns and ammunition for the Zionist paramilitary movement, Haganah, to quickly dispose of them.

While the weapons were thrown overboard, the passengers stayed below deck, silent, hoping that they would not be discovered, that the British would not board their boat. But soon they heard the sounds of a boat drawing alongside and heavy footsteps overhead. The footsteps were followed by voices ordering them to assemble on deck.

Every passenger was afraid of being sent back. With their food having run out, they were desperate not to have to endure another two-week journey and one that would be extra distressing for these desperate Jewish refugees who had come so far and so close to the shores of the Holy Land.

When she reached the upper deck, Zisi saw some British soldiers helping themselves to the last of the refugees' chocolate rations, having broken the lock of the food cabinet. Luckily, after a search, they found no traces of the guns intended for the Haganah.

Emotions were running high among the passengers, several of whom fainted. Zisi began to worry about her shoe that had come off in the rush to get up on deck. Then, some of the refugees began singing *Hatikva*, the Zionist song of longing for the homeland, which would later become the national anthem of the state of Israel. Within seconds, the singing spread to the entire mass of passengers.

Then the Enso Sereni began moving again, towards Haifa, the British vessel closely following. As they arrived at the dockside, exhausted, relieved and anxiously wondering what was going to happen to them, they saw hundreds of people cheering and waving. As they disembarked, they were met with cries of support: "Don't be afraid! You are home now!"

Zisi hobbled off the boat, weeping and wearing just one shoe. But her tears quickly turned to laughter as several shoes were passed to her from the crowd. While the refugees were told to wait for transport that would take them to a nearby prison, their spirits were lifted by the exuberant crowd of well-wishers, who passed them small packages of fruit and chocolate.

Once aboard the bus that would take them to the Atlit detention camp, Zisi peered out of the window to look at the landscape that she had travelled so far to see. And there were the much talked-about, pineapple-shaped palm trees, shading the road, as the bus made its way towards Atlit. To Zisi's left stood the green Carmel Mountains and on her right was the warm blue sea. Along the way, people – including many children – waved flags in greeting.

The detention camp was a short drive away and presented a shocking sight reminiscent of the horrors the refugees had left behind them – barbed-wire fences, barracks, and watchtowers in each corner. Huddled together, afraid, the bedraggled bunch of arrivals cried out in horror as they entered a large room and were asked to strip, shower and go through the delousing process.

But once they had come through the showers and the delousing, they were given back their clothes along with a choice of additional clean clothes. They began to relax after being given hot food and orange juice, and meeting other Jewish inmates who reassured them that this was a far cry from the Nazi camps. Indeed, after their initial, horrified reaction to being placed in yet another prison camp, Zisi and the others came to regard Atlit as a welcome relief from the cramped conditions of the boat – and the difficult trek across Europe that preceded it.

Zisi's partisan friends were all too familiar with prison life, having been in and out of jails for several years, and they immediately made themselves at home. Zisi couldn't share their easy acclimatisation to being incarcerated but she was very pleased to have a bed of her own and, finally, to be in Palestine.

The days passed quickly enough, with various activities organised by the Jewish Agency to prepare the new arrivals for life in Israel, as well as teach them Hebrew. Zisi no longer worried about being sent back to Europe and was confident that they would be able to put behind them the cruelty and persecution they and their families had suffered. She spent hours discussing with her housemates from Ostia what they would do once they left Atlit. They spoke about the possibility of kibbutz life, of working in the fields and, above all, of freedom. Friday nights in Atlit were particularly memorable, as they would be treated to special, big portions of schnitzel and potato salad, supplied by the local Jewish co-operative settlements, the kibbutzim.

Under the British Mandate in Palestine at that time, a certain number of refugees was allowed into the country each month. After three weeks in Atlit, it was the turn of Zisi and her companions. They were free. Representatives of Hashomer Hatzair came to help them adapt to their new situation and organised the former detainees into groups. Most of Zisi's friends were to be sent to Kibbutz Kfar Masaryk in Western Galilee but her destination was to Kibbutz Gat, to the south. Once again, she faced a round of emotional goodbyes.

For Zisi, new beginnings meant a new name. Zisi (or Metouka) seemed childish, so she decided to become Naomi (meaning pleasant). On the bus to Kibbutz Gat, she gazed through the window, transfixed by the landscape and the people. Palestine, she soon appreciated, was not populated simply by European Jewish refugees like herself. She was fascinated to see the diversity of the population and the different styles of dress of the native Jews and Arabs. As they drove further south, the terrain changed, the green trees gave way to the brown and sandy tones of the Negev desert.

The newcomers received a friendly welcome at Kibbutz Gat and were fed and allocated a dormitory room. The weather was warm and pleasant and Zisi, introducing herself as Naomi, looked forward to being part of a community again. In the morning, they were woken early to work in the *refet* (cow sheds) milking the cows – later Naomi was given work in the kitchens. She rose to the challenge of the work and enjoyed the camaraderie with her fellow refugees. Once they had completed their work shift, they would all meet in the communal dining room for lunch and then, after resting in the afternoon, would spend the evenings together.

After so much deprivation, Naomi was finding it hard to adapt to regular eating. She would be so hungry that she would fill her plate to excess, worried that she would not have anything to eat later when she might have hunger pangs again. But she was unable to consume the pile of food in front of her and it went to waste. Half-an-hour later, she would be hungry again. In order to quell her hunger, she filled her pockets with bread from the communal basket while the kibbutz members were not looking. Then, outside the dining room, she would find a hiding place where she would be able to eat the bread.

After a while, she discovered that most, if not all, of her friends were doing the same as her, filling themselves with bread in the grounds of the kibbutz. The veteran kibbutz members soon realised why there was so little bread in the bread baskets at meal-times and explained to the new arrivals that they had no need to hoard bread as there was always plenty of food.

After about a week, Naomi was placed with one of the kibbutz families. Despite the busy kibbutz schedule, with lectures and dancing in the evening designed to integrate the newcomers, Naomi did not feel comfortable. The rigid timekeeping, the meticulous organisation and lack of personal space fuelled her desire to study, to improve herself and to be free to organise her own life.

During Naomi's time at Gat, word reached as far as Jerusalem that the granddaughter of David Schlussel, the head of the beth din in Mukačevo, was living on a left-wing Hashomer kibbutz. And one day the kibbutzniks were bemused to see a strictly orthodox, Chasidic Jew arrive at the kibbutz asking for Zisel Düm. He announced rather grandly that he was there as an envoy of the Satmar Rebbe and told Naomi that they would help her find a place to live away from this kibbutz, which he and his fellow Chasidim viewed as the antithesis of Jewish tradition.

Though Naomi was not planning to stay permanently on the kibbutz, she certainly had no desire to live with the Satmar Chasidim. But even before she could decline his offer, the kibbutzniks, offended by the religious visitor's open distaste for their non-religious community, and keen to keep its new member, asked him to leave.

But, after three weeks, Naomi decided to move on. She made her way north to Tel Aviv, where she knew nobody and spent the night on the beach. The following day, she continued her journey to find her cousin Udi Kopolovitch who she had heard was living in Kfar Haroeh, a religious *moshav* – agricultural co-operative – 60 km north of Tel Aviv. Here she received news from Sari and Erno, still in Kosice, and from Malchi and Shimi, now living in Tangiers. They told her that Moishe was in Venezuela, trying to get a visa to enter the US and Ruchtu was in Brussels staying with their Uncle Heskel.

Her cousin, who lived alone, made her feel at home and she stayed with him for a few days, happy to be with family again. Udi advised her on finding places to live, work and eventually study. Her first port-of-call after Kfar Haroeh was Mikveh Israel, an agricultural school near Tel Aviv, which needed people to work in the kitchens. Here Naomi found immediate employment in exchange for a salary, ample food and a place to sleep. Now, at last, she told herself, she could control her life.

22

She would stand outside the apartment building and make sure the bus waited for Naomi while she finished dressing and drank her coffee

Working hard in the kitchens kept Naomi busy by day and sleeping in small tents with the other workers kept her entertained at night. She was able to put money aside for her studies and life was good – she even met somebody from Mukačevo, who was able to give her news of other friends. She heard that Shlomo and Moishe had both arrived safely in Palestine; Shlomo was living on a kibbutz in the north and Moishe was with his two sisters in Holon. Similarly her cousin Zishka, from whom she had been separated in Auschwitz, was also safely installed on a kibbutz in the South. Finally she heard, with much relief, that Chaya had recovered in Budapest and was on her way to Palestine.

After about a week at Mikveh Israel, Naomi received a visitor – again, a Chasid. It was a blazing hot day and the man was incongruously dressed in a black suit, black coat and hat. He announced himself in Yiddish and said he had come to see Zisi Düm, introducing himself as "Yechezkel Green". This was Naomi's mother's first cousin, who had left Mukačevo before the war with his family and had been living in Mea Shearim, in Jerusalem, ever since. Initially somewhat suspicious that he might be another envoy from the Satmar Rebbe, Naomi soon relaxed and warmed to the genuine family connection. She and her newly discovered relative exchanged stories and discussed Naomi's plans and hopes. He was kind and patient and, after hearing about her wish to study, invited her to come and stay with his family. "Our home is your home," he told her.

Naomi's first reaction was a polite refusal. She no longer felt she could live by the rules of a religious community; she wanted to be free to make her own decisions. But, after a second visit from Green, two weeks later, and the realisation that perhaps cleaning pots and pans was not the most demanding occupation, she started to consider his offer seriously. As on the previous occasion, he was warm and friendly and Naomi recognised more than just an elderly religious man. Moved by his kindness, his interest in secular Israel and his open-minded approach towards Naomi and her desire to study, she found herself tempted by the opportunity to be in Jerusalem.

And so, one month after arriving in Mikveh Yisrael, Naomi quit her job and went to the Greens' apartment. Here, she was greeted by Yechezkel, his wife and their three children. It turned out that her cousin was a fishmonger and the first meal that Naomi sat down to eat with them consisted of fish that Yechezkel had brought home from his shop.

The Greens' daughter, Zipora, lived at home and her two married brothers lived close by. Naomi felt immediately at home with this family and the Greens treated her like a second daughter and were never judgmental about her non-religious ways. Naomi respected their way of life and never discussed her ideas with them or their daughter.

On Shabbat, Naomi enjoyed watching her cousin setting off for the synagogue, dressed like a king in his white kaftan, *talit* (prayer shawl) and *shtreimel* (large, round, fur hat), bringing back memories of her father and grandfather. During the week, however, she found herself drawn away from the religious Mea Shearim district, to explore the streets and alleys of the city of Jerusalem and its university on the top of Mount Scopus.

News in the tightly-knit community travelled fast and when it was known in Mea Shearim that the non-religious granddaughter of the head of the Mukačevo beth din was living there, Naomi was visited several times by the wife of the Satmar Rebbe. On each occasion, she came laden with clothing and gifts for Naomi and invited her to join her at prayer or at women's meetings. Wary of the attention given to her and determined to remain independent and follow her secular beliefs, Naomi respectfully turned down these offers of companionship and involvement in the community.

Yechezkel respected Naomi's need for independence and helped her to find a job locally – in a small shop making lampshades. With her pay from this job and some money that she received from time to time from Malchi and Shimi in Tangiers, she was able and ready to leave the confines of religious Mea Shearim and find a place of her own in Jerusalem.

Her first stop in the search for somewhere to live was Beit Hachalutzot, in the Rehavia district, a hostel run by the Jewish Agency for new female immigrants who were alone in Palestine. There was a long waiting-list, however, and after putting her name on the list, Naomi moved on. She went to the nearby offices of the Jewish Agency, where she was offered a job working for a dentist called Dr Gassman. For a few hours a day, she would clean his office and surgery, including all his medical instruments, and then go on to the shop making lampshades.

She heard about a vacant room in Geula, on the east side of Jerusalem, but when she got to the address in Rashi Street, the room was no longer available. However, seeing her disappointment, the owner suggested another solution. He took her into the lobby of the apartment building and down a couple of steps under the stairs, where there was a small corridor, approximately three-and-a-half metres long by two metres wide, with a door at each end and a small window high up on one side. Naomi immediately claimed it as her own. After two-and-a-half months in Palestine, she had secured both work and a home.

With the help of friends and some of the families in the building, Naomi furnished her little corridor with a bed, chair and desk. Through the Jewish Agency and some friends, she obtained blankets, towels, a lamp and additional items of clothing.

During the day, Naomi would leave open the door to her little home in order to get some natural light, allowing the children in the building to peep inside. The families in the apartments took a liking to this happy, smiling newcomer who demanded so little. Knowing of the terrible life she had endured in Europe, they looked out for her and helped her wherever possible. One woman would prepare her a cup of hot, sweet coffee every morning at 8 o'clock while Naomi was hastily getting dressed.

Furthermore, this neighbour would stand outside the apartment building and make sure the bus waited for Naomi while she finished dressing and drank her coffee. After a few days, the driver and passengers became so accustomed to this scene that the driver would sound his horn as he was turning the corner into Rashi Street, to warn Naomi that he was pulling up outside the building. The passengers seemed quite content to wait for her to finish her coffee before boarding the bus to Dr Gassman's office in Rehavia. On Shabbat, the same thoughtful neighbour would gently knock on Naomi's door to offer her a plate of couscous.

Despite the size of Naomi's little home, she was never alone. Friends and neighbours were always visiting and somehow she always found room for them on the bed, table, floor or chair. In July 1946, Naomi was accepted on to a preparatory course at the Hebrew University. Having missed out on her education because of the war, she had a lot of catching up to do. She also had to work hard at her language studies, as all lessons at the university would be in Hebrew.

Once she began her studies, Naomi was forced to leave the lampshade shop. From this point on, she relied on the few hours' work at Dr Gassman's and additional part-time jobs that she found with the help of the Jewish Agency. The first of these jobs was as a cleaner, with many sheets to wash. Inexperienced in this type of work, Naomi soon began to suffer from red,

raw hands and knuckles, from scrubbing the sheets together. Her skin started peeling and the flesh was painful when she put her hands in water. The
next day, she went to work with her hands bandaged. She was asked to leave
within a week.

During this period, Naomi became particularly close to a young, native
Israeli poet. She loved to hear him read his poetry to her, which he did will-
ingly and often. He wrote several poems to her and about her – including
one about her bandaged hands. He was clearly devoted to Naomi but she
was far too busy meeting her wide circle of friends, and entertaining them
in her little corridor room, to become involved with one person.

Soon after moving to Rashi Street, Naomi also received news from
Chaya, who had arrived in Palestine and was living on Kibbutz Yasur,
training to be a nursery teacher. Naomi immediately wrote to her and, as
soon as she was able, travelled to see her for an emotional reunion. Chaya,
like Naomi, had been taken with her mother and two sisters to Auschwitz.
Her mother, Mathilde, and her younger sister, Ada, had not survived and
Chaya had been separated from her older sister Rachel and sent to work in
a munitions factory near Auschwitz. There she survived the war and after
she was liberated she spent several months recovering from a severe lung
infection in Budapest. Once recovered, Chaya joined the Hashomer activities in
Bucharest – just as Naomi had done some months earlier – to prepare for
kibbutz life, reaching Palestine in 1946.

Naomi and Chaya resumed their friendship mainly by writing to each other
and with the occasional visit. Naomi also liked to travel on her days off,
visiting her partisan friends in Kfar Masaryk, in particular, Chana Blonder,
her cousin Udi in Kfar Haroeh and her mother's cousin in Mea Shearim.
On one such visit to Kfar Haroeh, Udi, to Naomi's great surprise, proposed
marriage. Thinking he was joking, she laughed. In any event, she did not
want to take the risk of marrying a family member – or anybody else at
this point. She was in love with Jerusalem, her little home, her friends, her
neighbours and her independence. She had all the time in the world.

23

*After three nights of sleeping end to end in Naomi's narrow bed,
the two of them were exhausted from lack of sleep and sore
from kicking each other*

At Naomi's first evening class for the Hebrew University preparatory course, in October 1946, she found herself surrounded by *Sabras* – native Israelis. Conscious of her poor Hebrew and foreign accent, she smiled silently at everyone. When the lesson began, a slender, pretty young woman stood up to ask some questions. While the Sabras laughed as the woman tried to make herself understood in less-than-perfect Hebrew, Naomi recognised the Hungarian accent. And, when it was her turn to speak, she felt strangely comforted to know that there was someone else like her in the room. She hardly noticed the renewed laughter prompted by her own Hungarian accent.

The other Hungarian speaker was Chana Aczel, who had arrived in Israel from Hungary in November 1944 with the Youth Aliyah children's charity. Chana's mother and brother had been murdered in a concentration camp; her father had survived and was living in Budapest. During the war she worked with the Jewish underground in Budapest before being captured on the Romanian border and imprisoned. When the Russians entered Romania in September 1944 she made her way to Bucharest and from there to Palestine.

Naomi and Chana became close friends in a short space of time, studying and socialising together. At that time, Chana was lodging in the Talpiot district of Jerusalem with Chemda Ben Yehuda, widow of Eliezer Ben Yehuda, the principal instigator of the revival and establishment of the Hebrew language in the modern Jewish state. Chana was given a room rent-free in the Ben Yehuda house, next to a British army barracks, in exchange for acting as Chemda's companion. Naomi visited frequently and the two girls spent much of their time there, studying or just enjoying each other's company.

One evening while Chemda was out, Naomi and Chana were studying on the balcony of the second floor of the house. Next door, on the barrack roof, a bunch of Scottish soldiers were having a party. When they saw the two young women, the men tried to draw them into a conversation, but the girls were having none of it. This only made the soldiers, who had been drinking quite heavily, intensify their efforts. They tried to climb up to the balcony and Naomi and Chana watched in horror as the soldiers slipped off the wall and fell over themselves several times.

The next morning, at the bus stop, these same young men respectfully stood aside for Chana to board the bus and revealed no sign or memory of the previous night's escapade.

The bus that took Chana to and from the centre of town was the number seven. It was not always a pleasant journey. Next to the bus stop in town was a bar much frequented by the army and, going home at night, Chana would find herself nervously sharing the bus with inebriated soldiers as they travelled to the barracks. As a child, Chana had witnessed drunken thugs attacking Jews on the streets of her home town Székesfehérvár, and now in Jerusalem she was feeling the legacy of anxiety. She always made sure not to sit alone and would far prefer to sit with the Arab men, also travelling to their homes in Talpiot, than with the soldiers. The cultural distance between Jews and Arabs and their respect for women made her feel considerably more secure.

Chana enjoyed Chemda's company but gradually found that the older woman was becoming too dependent on her. One evening, just as Chana was leaving for her class, Chemda complained of pain, saying that she had a weak heart and was frightened of being left alone. The same thing happened, at exactly the same time, the next evening, and the next. After missing several classes, Chana decided that she had to leave.

Naomi pleaded with Chana to come and share her little corridor on Rashi Street. With little enough room there even to sleep on the floor, however, Chana dismissed this offer. Instead, she managed to find another rent-free lodging, this time in exchange for looking after the baby of a single mother. But when she arrived at the mother's home, it transpired that she would not have a room of her own, just a small sofa in the corner of the one-room apartment.

After just one sleepless night, Chana turned up on Naomi's doorstep. And now she was persuaded to stay in Naomi's small but cosy room. After three nights end to end in one narrow bed, though, the two of them were exhausted from lack of sleep and sore from kicking each other. So they came up with a new plan. From nine o'clock in the evening until two in the morning, Naomi would sleep and Chana would study at the table. At two, Chana would take Naomi's place in bed and Naomi would study for the rest of the night. At daybreak, the two would rise, wash in a bowl of water brought in from the courtyard and, with no time or money for food, they would leave for their respective workplaces and meet at the class in the evening.

Chana and Naomi both struggled with their studies. Neither had been able to finish high school back home and, of course, neither had been exposed to the Jewish school system in Palestine. Naomi's education had been interrupted at the age of 15 when Jews were banned from going to school. But she had received a strong Jewish and religious education, even learning some Hebrew with Hashomer Hatzair. Chana had attended agricultural school on arrival in Israel but her schooling, too, was incomplete and she had very little religious education.

Jewish history and religious studies were therefore not difficult for Naomi to absorb but maths, physics, chemistry and Hebrew were. The two girls' expectations that they could make up 12 years of study in just a few months were clearly too optimistic but they did their utmost to succeed and supported each other.

With the help of the Jewish Agency, they were never without work – cleaning, looking after children or performing clerical jobs in small businesses. But, with tuition fees taking up half their earnings, they barely had enough left for rent, food and bus fares. Yet these were happy days, when they entertained friends in the confines of the corridor room. There were no cooking facilities but the local grocer allowed them to buy milk, oranges, bread and cheese on credit.

In due course, a place became available for Chana at Beit Hachalutzot women's hostel. She was reluctant to leave the little room at first, so strong had the bond with Naomi become. But it really was too small and so she departed for the hostel. Naomi was content to stay in the corridor, close to her neighbours and friends – and especially one new friend.

She had met Zvi in a bag shop, where he was working behind the till. He was tall, with a charming smile and voice and the attraction was mutual. He invited her out to the cinema and she readily accepted. But Naomi remained convinced that she was not yet ready for a serious relationship and Zvi, too, had a wide circle of female friends. Nevertheless, there was something special between them.

Following Chana's departure from Rashi Street, Naomi began to feel restless in her small home. Her open-door policy was beginning to backfire; she would often come home tired and find friends, or some of the local children, waiting in her room. Although she never turned people away, she had little privacy and not enough time to study.

She wanted to cut down on her paid work to give herself more studying time, but couldn't afford to. She would really have liked to join Chana at Beit Hachalutzot. But there was still no room. Used to restricted living space, Naomi said she would be willing to stay in Beit Hachalutzot's small loft, used for washing and ironing. The warden agreed and Naomi was allowed to set up a small bed there behind a curtain, until a proper room became free. Although the loft room was in use during the day, at night Naomi had it to herself and was able to focus on her studies.

But it wasn't long before one of the girls in Chana's room left and Naomi was allowed to take her place. Delighted to be back with Chana again, along with her other two room-mates, Etu and Dvora, Naomi soon felt at home. All four girls were trying to balance work and studies, and supported each other generously.

Etu, who was born in Mukačevo, was the oldest. Training to be a nurse, she always had time for everyone's problems. Her kind and attentive manner encouraged others to confide in her and she was a source of great strength to many of the girls in Beit Hachalutzot, not least Naomi, Chana and Dvora. Dvora, also from Hungary, was a lively girl with a beautiful singing voice. She studied Bible at the Hebrew University but often suffered from ill health, later diagnosed as leukaemia.

With Chana and Naomi always busy studying, socialising and working, the four room-mates looked out for each other, counselled each other and knew everything about each other – or almost everything. Settling into this more affordable and comfortable living situation gave each one of them the time and strength to join the clandestine activities of the Haganah, about which they shared only minimal information.

It also gave them the opportunity to make new friendships and strengthen old ones. Etu met a young man called Amram; Dvora had become very attached to Bondi and Chana became fond of a young man called Ezra. Naomi found time to visit Moishe and his sisters, Rivka and Shoshi, who were living in Holon, and began to develop a close friendship with Shoshi but most of all she continued to enjoy the company of her new friend, Zvi.

24

*"We danced – but we knew that ahead of us lay the
battlefields" (Moshe Dayan, 1976)*

Naomi's studies at the university coincided with a period of increased tension in Palestine between Arabs and Jews. The British army was there to
prevent serious hostilities, but seemed ineffective – or indifferent. The attitude among British army personnel seemed to be one of "a plague on both
their houses". With increased guerrilla activity going on around them, Naomi
sensed the unease among Jews in Jerusalem and, in early 1947, when the
Haganah stepped up its recruiting drive among young people, she signed up
for its officer training course.

Both sides were seeking to establish territorial strongholds before the
awaited United Nations debate on Palestine, in advance of any decision to
partition the land – or indeed of all-out war.

Naomi's first spell of training was a two-week course in Kibbutz Ma'ale
Hahamisha, where both men and women were put through a tough
regime. Every morning, the recruits had to run six kilometres. Apart from
a very few fit females, Naomi and the other women found this run very
difficult and it was a little humiliating when they staggered back to find the
men already comfortably sitting at breakfast.

During the course, Naomi befriended a woman officer, Batsheva Shinhar,
an experienced soldier who had trained in the British Army. Batsheva was
impressed by Naomi's enthusiasm and ability to engage with others and
talked to her about becoming a full-time soldier. Intent on continuing
her studies, Naomi was reluctant, but she agreed to join the Palmach, the
Haganah's elite fighting force, as a convoy escort – *melavah shayarot*.

Fierce fighting was taking place on the road between Jerusalem and Tel
Aviv and armoured cars were regularly sent to Tel Aviv to bring food supplies and ammunition. Naomi was deputed to undertake such deliveries, to

help keep open the lines of communication – a task that terrified her, she admitted to Chana, because she did not want to shoot anyone. Later she was also assigned to a group of fighters stationed in Yemin Moshe to resist Arab attacks on the area.

Along with four other young recruits, she spent several days at a time guarding this position from behind a small barricade, while Arab guerrillas took pot shots at them, right under the eyes of the British army. With one rifle between them, Naomi and her comrades remained quietly behind a wall of sandbags. The rifle, which needed to be concealed from investigating British soldiers, was rarely used as they had very little ammunition.

As the tension increased between the two sides, Naomi found herself having to take more and more time out of her studies. Her room-mates never asked any questions when she failed to come home, just as she never asked when they disappeared for several hours on end, all with their own endeavours to help the cause. During this time, Chana moved to a small room of her own in Romema and, against the background of impending war and her own duties in the Haganah, she and Ezra talked of marriage.

By the end of October 1947, with the UN decision imminent and tensions rising, more and more young people abandoned their studies and joined the Haganah, in the expectation of a war. If the UN did not agree to partition Palestine into two states, one Jewish and one Palestinian, then the Jews would continue to have little control over their destiny. If it did grant partition, this would be a glorious moment in Jewish history, but it would almost certainly meet with defiance from Arab nations and trigger a war.

As the UN resolution approached, in November 1947, Naomi decided to go north to Kibbutz Kfar Masaryk and visit her friend Chana Blonder and the other partisans with whom she had lived in Italy. Having struggled so hard with these people to reach Palestine, she felt it would be fitting to be with them when the UN decision was announced. On November 29, the whole kibbutz gathered in the communal dining room to listen to the announcement on the radio; each country's UN representative stating, one after the other, whether they were for or against the partition. With the "yes" vote of the Philippines, the Israeli Jews knew that they had enough votes for a majority but, in the Kfar Masaryk dining hall, they dared not celebrate until the final announcement: "Thirty-three votes for partition, thirteen against and ten abstentions." Suddenly, the dining hall became the scene, replicated all over the country, of rapturous, emotional celebrations. All day and all night long, the kibbutz members danced around campfires, sang and rejoiced, putting out of their minds for the time being the war that would inevitably follow.

The sentiments of the Jews of Palestine on that day are described in the autobiography of General Moshe Dayan, who at the time of the UN vote was a senior officer in the Haganah. Writing almost 30 years later, as Israel's Minister of Defence, he recollected:

"I felt in my bones the victory of Judaism, which for two thousand years of exile from the Land of Israel had withstood persecutions, the Spanish Inquisition, pogroms, anti-Jewish decrees, restrictions, and the mass slaughter by the Nazis in our own generation, and had reached the fulfilment of its age-old yearning – the return to a free and independent Zion.

"We were happy that night, and we danced, and our hearts went out to every nation whose UN representative had voted in favour of the resolution. We had heard them utter the magic word 'yes' as we followed their voices over the airwaves from thousands of miles away. We danced – but we knew that ahead of us lay the battlefields."

Despite the threat by other Arab nations to take up arms against the newly created state, the UN decision instilled confidence in the Jews of Israel. Their cause had been recognised, their right to sovereignty had been recognised, and their army would be recognised – and reckoned with. Now, they had a future to fight for. An excited Naomi Düm returned from Kfar Masaryk determined to play her part.

Following the UN decision, the Jewish population found itself increasingly under attack from small Arab militias. The British were to remain in a peace-keeping role in Palestine until the end of the Mandate in May 1948. They were, however, unable to exert much control and their attention appeared to be directed, above all, towards their departure from this area of apparently intractable hostilities.

Although an official Jewish army was still not permitted and the supply of weapons was severely limited by the British, the Haganah grew in numbers and soon became more resourceful in developing its own weapons.

25

Many of the bodies were burnt beyond identification

As the shadow of war deepened over the next few months, university courses were suspended and Naomi spent far less time at Beit Hachalutzot. She saw little of Chana and Ezra, who married in December 1947 and lived in Chana's apartment in Romema. Etu, like Naomi, still kept a bed at Beit Hachaluztot but was away much of the time, carrying out her duties as a nurse. Dvora remained, however, as her poor health prevented her from being accepted into the Haganah.

Naomi's main duty was to lead the defence of her team's position in Yemin Moshe, where she had been appointed *mefakedet emda* (station commander). Now, more than ever, it was essential to strengthen their hold on significant areas of Jerusalem before the departure of the British, so as to retain an advantage if war broke out. But, with the British army watching over them and weapons limited, their task was difficult. All that Naomi and her colleagues could do was stay hidden behind their sandbags and try to give the impression that they were better armed than they actually were.

At the sight of any movement, Arab snipers would fire at them. Naomi's team needed to be very selective in returning the fire – and to do so in such a concentrated fashion as to appear capable of sustained firepower. Most days, Yemin Moshe was fairly quiet until around 5pm, when the Arab guerrilla attacks would begin. Fortunately for the defenders of Yemin Moshe, these attacks were poorly co-ordinated.

April 1, 1948 was a significant day for Naomi. As the tension rose with the increase in Arab attacks, she and her team felt constantly vulnerable. One morning – usually a quiet time – Naomi and some other station leaders were working together to devise an escape route, in case the Arab fighters managed to overrun the area. As they clambered up ridges and rolled into small dips looking for the safest way out, they noticed that they were being watched from all directions by the British army. Naomi looked up towards Mount Zion where she saw a British soldier tinkering with his gun. He looked back directly at Naomi and then aimed his rifle. She heard the shots and felt a barrage of stones and dust. The next thing she knew was that all her comrades were around her, supporting her as blood gushed from her neck.

She felt nothing except a strange vibration in her voice. When she tried to speak, no words would come out. Still able to walk and wondering what all the fuss was about, Naomi was escorted to a car that took her immediately to the Hadassah Hospital in the city centre. By the time she arrived, she had lost a lot of blood and could no longer stand.

The next 24 hours were a haze but, a few days later when Naomi was recovering, her friends told her what had happened. The British soldier's bullets had hit a rock and the shrapnel had ricocheted into her neck. Perhaps, they speculated, the soldier had been trying to fire a warning bullet, his way of telling her to stay low. For ten days, Naomi remained under observation at the hospital, not just by the medical staff but also by friends who took it in turns to sit with her and keep her informed of events outside.

Arab militias had cut off the only road between Tel Aviv and Jerusalem and the battle for Jerusalem itself had intensified. The siege of Jerusalem, which had begun the previous month and would last until June with only two short-lived breaches, was preventing food and ammunition from getting through. Consequently, the many casualties from the battle for Jerusalem and along the Jerusalem road put great pressure on the city's hospitals.

On April 12, Naomi and some other patients still in need of care and rest, were moved to another branch of Hadassah on Mount Scopus. This was connected to the city by a narrow access road, a mile-and-a-half long, which passed through a number of Arab villages. Traffic between the hospital and the city was vulnerable to attack and medical staff would always await British confirmation that the road was safe to travel.

Naomi was taken in a small ambulance with a handful of nurses and a few of the more stable patients. Despite Arab threats, the ambulance was granted safe passage and reached its destination safely. The team of doctors and nurses that Naomi had grown used to in town were due to arrive the following day in a large convoy, together with much-needed equipment and supplies. Throughout that next day, Naomi rested quietly, getting to know the other patients, but was impatient for the medical convoy to turn up. She was eager to see one of the nurses with whom she had developed a close friendship.

After several hours, news emerged over the radio – and from a survivor – that the convoy had been attacked. The small group of Haganah soldiers accompanying the convoy had been overwhelmed by bombs, grenades and

heavy gunfire. No help was getting through and, after several bombard-
ments, the six vehicles were surrounded by Arab militia. The intense fire
lasted for several hours, during which time Haganah aid was unable to
reach them. Finally, the fuel leaking from the vehicles was set alight and the
seven vehicles burned. Although British troops were only metres away, they
refused to intervene without direct orders from their superiors – which did
not come for seven hours, at which point the British soldiers fired heavy
rockets to disperse the militia and allow Haganah back-up to get through.

For many, including Naomi's nurse friend, it was too late. Seventy-seven
men and women in the convoy were dead and 47 remained unaccounted
for; many of the bodies were burnt beyond identification.

Following this attack, no more convoys could pass. There was no way to
send medical teams or supplies to Mount Scopus and there was no way
down for the patients. They were cut off from Jerusalem.

April 13 proved a fateful day in the history of the conflict, but also brought
bad news to Chana. So busy were Naomi and Chana with their respective
duties, that they had little contact in the weeks leading up to Naomi's injury.
Chana knew nothing of Naomi's condition and had also not heard from Ezra
for several days. Stricken with worry, on April 13 she was notified that Ezra
had been killed defending Jewish positions at Castel on the way to Jerusalem.

Unaware of Chana's tragic news and cut off from Etu, Dvora, Zvi and her
other dear friends throughout the country, Naomi had many hours to fill.
She was glad of the visits from Jewish soldiers on Mount Scopus and particularly pleased to find a familiar face among them. Dov Levine, a friend from
Jerusalem stationed at Scopus, often sat with her, especially in the evenings
when she was having dinner. Naomi ate very little as a result of her injuries
and Dov was always happy to finish her food.

In fact, everybody was eating very little. With no supplies getting through,
food was scarce. The patients were fed before the soldiers and so, even when
hungry, Naomi made sure she kept some back for Dov. In return, Dov
brought Naomi something that would prove invaluable – some olive wood
and a knife. For hours on end, Naomi found herself carving and sculpting
the wood into small statuettes and found that she was a natural. Her very
first sculpture was a little dog, to remind her of her own pet, Fidi, given to
her by her brother Fishel in Mukačevo. Little did she know that this activity,
born out of boredom and isolation, was the beginning of an artistic career.

26

Chana quickly pushed Naomi aside, took the wheel, and drove away

The attack on the Hadassah Hospital convoy signalled the end of Jewish occupation of Mount Scopus. Although the road linking Mount Scopus to the city centre was opened again, it was no longer considered safe to negotiate the route to Hadassah and it was decided that all equipment, patients and staff should be relocated to the centre of Jerusalem. With a large Haganah presence along the road and the guarantee of support from the British, three weeks after her arrival on Mount Scopus, Naomi returned to Jerusalem, almost fully recovered. She received a warm welcome at Beit Hachalutzot, where she was reunited with Etu and Dvora, who made sure that Naomi was able to recuperate fully. Not long afterwards, Chana also returned, still in shock at the death of Ezra, but as determined and active as ever. The three were together again.

With the Jerusalem-Tel Aviv Road still cut off despite numerous attempts by Jewish fighters to regain control at Latrun and Castel, conditions in Jerusalem had become precarious. Without supplies of fresh food, water and medical equipment, people were struggling. Water, in particular, had to be rationed. Long queues became a familiar sight. Etu was characteristically resourceful; from her, Naomi and Chana learned how to wash using a small amount of water on a piece of cotton wool, then to squeeze the cotton wool into a jug and use half for the dishes and half to wash the floor.

Life was dangerous as well as difficult, as fighting continued in many parts of the city. The British were slowly preparing to leave Palestine and their "peace-keeping" involvement was now quite sporadic. The real battle was about to begin. Everyone was awaiting May 15, the date of final British withdrawal, with trepidation. There was debate among Jerusalem's Jewish inhabitants about how they could and should react. To take the initiative and declare their independence as a state would risk extending the conflict beyond the Palestinian Arabs into the five neighbouring Arab countries and quite possibly facing defeat at the state's very birth. The alternative was to accept a three-month ceasefire while the US tried to find a political solution and allow the UN to take control.

With no firm evidence that a full UN force would be set up within Palestine in time and little reassurance that the ceasefire would be honoured, Israel's founding Prime Minister, David Ben Gurion and his cabinet chose to declare an independent state of Israel and legitimise the Israel Defence Forces. After 2,000 years, the dream had become a reality, but the celebrations were muted – Israel was on the brink of war.

The Declaration of Independence brought about the integration of the various Jewish fighting units into one official, organised army. As more people joined the army, so the organisational tasks grew. Buildings were converted into army barracks and the streets were thronged with people in uniform. Etu continued her nursing training in military hospitals and Chana was put in charge of army recruits in the Shneller Barracks, not far from Beit Hachalutzot. As for Naomi, she was itching to return to army duties. As soon as she was well enough, she began work in one of the offices in the Shneller Barracks, where she was visited by her Haganah officer friend, Batsheva Shinar. Batsheva was now an officer in the 205th Women's Corps Battalion and invited Naomi to work with her to manage a division of 100 women based at Shneller. Naomi needed no persuading and promptly embarked on an officer's training course – along with Chana.

Chana, however, had found managing a group of female soldiers frustrating and she asked to be transferred to a different position, training young male soldiers instead of the "childish" females in her control. In the event, she was given instruction as a military truck driver.

When she had completed her training, Chana was keen to show her new driving skills to Naomi and took her for a drive around Jerusalem in a small vehicle used for chauffeuring senior officers. After a short time, Naomi asked Chana to teach her to drive. The two girls thought it would be fun for Naomi to have a go at the wheel. But it wasn't. Within moments, Naomi crashed into a stationary bus. Chana quickly pushed Naomi aside, took the wheel, and drove away. Luckily for them, they weren't seen. It was some years before Naomi took up driving again.

Having completed her officer training, Naomi was placed in command of the group of 100 women, reporting directly to Batsheva. She was responsible for co-ordinating and organising the duties and activities of the women in her charge and supervising their fitness and training. The post required Naomi to live at Shneller, where she and Batsheva shared a room. She was allowed to maintain her room at Beit Hachalutzot but went back there only on her days off; for several months Shneller became her home. The women in her charge worked mainly in administrative jobs at the barracks but were often sent to assist in other areas of Jerusalem. Although they were not involved in direct combat, they were asked to undertake dangerous and confidential missions and therefore their discipline and training were of the utmost importance. Naomi and Batsheva would often travel to monitor the safety and conduct of their soldiers while on these missions.

Along with the privations in terms of food and money, winters could be harsh in Jerusalem. Warm clothing was expensive – though Naomi was given a British army blanket. She also managed, with Chana's help, to find a tailor who agreed to make her a coat from the blanket material at very little expense. Such small acts of kindness helped Naomi get through cold nights training her young soldiers in the open air and visiting those of her division based in more remote locations.

Despite the siege and the desperate nature of the war, the spirits of the girls at Shneller were high. Naomi, as friend and officer of these girls, had to work hard to maintain their positive attitude on the one hand and their discipline on the other. This was particularly challenging as Naomi's injury had substantially weakened her voice.

One night, Naomi and Batsheva were woken by screaming in one of the rooms where their young charges slept. Fearing the worst, they ran into the room – to find the women inside hysterical with laughter. Some of their peers had sneaked into the room, dressed in white sheets and making scary, ghost noises.

Sometimes, when a recruit did not wake up on time, Naomi would order the culprit's comrades to bring her out, in her bed, to roll-call. She dealt with most instances of disorder with humour and goodwill. Despite her inability to raise her voice, she gained the trust and respect of her charges and by the end of 1948 was promoted to the rank of sub-lieutenant.

It turned out that Zvi – the man from the bag shop in Geula to whom Naomi had formed an attachment – was also stationed at Shneller, managing the equipment and uniform store. They managed to spend a lot of time together – though Naomi did sense a twinge of resentment on his part at her officer status.

In the evenings, when not on duty, Zvi and Naomi went the cinema and shared their interest in music and opera. Zvi had a good tenor voice and took private lessons. His teacher believed he had great potential and during periods of ceasefire arranged for him to appear in many concerts – with Naomi always in the audience to give him support.

In October 1948, following the failure of two ceasefires, a third one was agreed. The small nation had suffered numerous casualties but they were slowly managing to fight off their attackers. Although a global ceasefire was not to last in the South of the country, a sincere ceasefire was declared in Jerusalem in November. During this time soldiers remained at their bases on alert but no action occurred. This gave Naomi and her friends time and space to speculate about the future. Naomi and Chana talked of continuing their studies. Zvi's ambition was to train in Italy to become an opera singer.

Fighting continued on the southern borders with Egypt, accompanied by fierce attempts by the UN to achieve a lasting truce. Finally, in February 1949, a ceasefire was agreed and over the next six months an armistice was signed with each of the neighbouring Arab states. Naomi was no longer needed in the army and she returned for a short period to Beit Hachalutzot, where she was reunited only briefly with Etu and Chana. By then, Etu had become a fully fledged nurse and met a young man called Amram. It was not long before she moved out of Beit Hachalutzot and married him. Chana also decided to move to a small apartment in the centre of town where she could concentrate on her studies.

Although Naomi, too, tried to continue her studies, she had missed a lot more schooling than Chana and felt unable to make up so much lost time. She decided not to sit the entrance exams. Chana continued and was accepted as a "non-matriculation" student, whereby she could study certain subjects but not attain a degree.

By now, Naomi's mind was focused on a different future. Zvi suggested that she move into the apartment in Moshava Germanit that came with his army job. They talked about going to Italy together to enable him to develop his talent. A couple of months later, and against the better judgment of her friends, Naomi agreed to marry Zvi and go with him to Rome. The ceremony was performed by an army rabbi in Batsheva's garden with a small group of friends in attendance. Four weeks later, they set off for Rome.

Here they found a room in Giulio Cesare Street and Zvi began his training. For all the excitement of being in Rome again, Naomi's enthusiasm soon wore off as she found it difficult to find work and spent much of her time alone. Zvi became more and more involved in his new life and career and kept late nights. Then, when he arrived home, he would tell Naomi about his huge success and boast of how all the young women admired him.

In an uncertain state of mind and longing to see her sisters who were also living in Europe, Naomi took a trip to Brussels, where Ruchtu lived – she had married their Uncle Heskel – and where Naomi would be able to consult a well-known doctor about her voice, which was still very weak. After staying a short while with Ruchtu, she continued to Morocco, for an emotional reunion with Malchi.

Naomi 1946

Below: Naomi with
Chaya 1946

Naomi's cousin Zishka,
Israel 1947

Below: Chana Blonder and
husband

Opposite, top: Naomi with
Chana 1949

Opposite below, left: Zvi
1949

Opposite below, right:
Naomi 1948

Shari & Pishta 1963

Below, left: Chana 1946

Below, right: Etu 1948

Opposite, top: Naomi 1949

Opposite, below: Naomi with
Dvora 1953

Left: Asher 1945

Below: Naomi and Asher in Florence 1952

Opposite; Asher with his daughter Helen

Opposite, below: Naomi and Asher on their engagement in 1953

Playa de Aro
1962

Naomi and Asher with Anita
on their 40th Wedding Anniversary

Helen and her family 1987. From
left to right: Eli, Gidi, Ruti, Tamar,
Sharon, Helen and Ido

Opposite, top left: Naomi and
Asher 1961

Opposite right: Naomi with Asher,
Jonathan and Anita 1962

Above: Naomi with Shoshi 2007

Left: Naomi with Chaya 2007

Below; Naomi with Chana 2007

Opposite, top: Naomi with the whole family 2012

Opposite, below: Naomi with grandchildren; from left to right Mikey, Simon, David, Lucy and Ben

View Bristol Cathedral
1980

Opposite: Naomi with
Embryo

Naomi with *Solitude*
1978

Below: Naomi with Lady
Elizabeth Maxwell and
Dr. Steven Smith at the
Unveiling of *Abandoned*
Beth Shalom Holocaust
Education Centre1991

Opposite: *Renew Our Days*
Sternberg Centre 1986

Naomi with *Family Group III*

She and Malchi – so close throughout the war – had kept in touch by letter. Malchi's husband Shimi was a shrewd businessman and the couple had successfully settled down in Tangier and started a family. By the time Naomi came to visit them, they had two young daughters, Ada and Zavi. Overjoyed, Naomi immediately felt at home with her sister and developed a close bond with her two nieces. The sisters shared news of relatives in Israel and around the world. Sari and Erno, who had two sons born in Kosice, had finally managed to emigrate to Sydney, Australia in 1949. Her brother Moishe was now settled in Venezuela and married to Rosa, expecting their first child and Fishel was in New York.

Naomi stayed for several months, during which she reflected a great deal on her marriage. She still loved Zvi but did not want to remain in Italy; she wanted to return to Israel. Zvi also missed Naomi and promised to return to Israel as soon as he had completed his operatic training. With this promise, Naomi eagerly set off back to Israel.

27

Herman was so excited to be speeding through the countryside that he didn't notice that Naomi had fallen off the back of the motorbike

In the spring of 1950 Naomi returned to Israel, to the little apartment that she and Zvi shared in Moshava Germanit and to Chana and her other friends. Before long – with the help of some of those friends – Naomi found a job at the Ministry of Commerce. She was initially interviewed by the head of the textile division for the position of secretary but her written Hebrew was not good enough. Wanting to help her, the head of the division pointed her in the direction of an area where good, written Hebrew was not essential – the statistics office, where she compiled and calculated data. She worked there happily for several months.

All the other women in the office spent much of the time chatting and gossiping. Naomi wasn't especially disposed to chit-chat and looked for odd jobs to keep her busy – such as organising files and tidying cupboards. This impressed one of her managers, who promoted her. Although she hadn't been competent enough in Hebrew to be a secretary, now she was given a secretary of her own!

At that time, Chana was still a student at the Hebrew University, working part-time in the university library and living in a small room in the centre of town. The two of them continued to spend a lot of time together. Times were still tough, with the effects of war and an influx of more than 600,000 Jewish immigrants between 1947 and 1951, and Israel struggled to build housing and provide food for its growing population.

One day, Chana excitedly announced that her father, Pishta and stepmother, Sari were about to arrive in Jerusalem from Hungary. Chana had not seen her father since May 1944. Pishta's first wife – Chana's mother – had lost her life in the war and he had subsequently married Sari, who was his wife's sister. Sari's first husband and two sons were also murdered in a concentration camp.

When Pishta and Sari arrived in Jerusalem in May 1950, Chana helped them to find a place to live in Moshava Germanit. They had very little money, so Chana decided to give up her studies and work full-time in order to help them. Luckily, there was a position available in the Ministry of Commerce, where Naomi was working, which Chana took gratefully.

Chana had taken Naomi to meet Sari and Pishta almost as soon as they set foot in Israel and they quickly formed a bond. Moreover, Sari's and Pishta's modest home soon became a regular Sabbath venue for lots of young visitors.

Meanwhile, Naomi was still waiting for Zvi to join her – although she kept up a full social life. She spent quite a bit of time with Herman, the brother of her Mukačevo childhood friend, Yitte. Naomi had heard that Yitte had died of leukaemia in Auschwitz but Herman had survived and made his way to Israel. He ran a small restaurant at the railway station and often invited Naomi to eat there.

Herman was kind, gentle and something of a character. He was a keen boxer and Naomi used to accompany him to bouts and act as his second, which involved washing him down between rounds. She did not enjoy wiping away his blood but, as his friend, she did not want to disappoint him.

One day, Herman turned up at Naomi's home unannounced and very excited. He asked her to come outside and proudly introduced her to his new motorbike, offering her the chance to be his first passenger. Again, this was not something that came easily to Naomi and, once they were out of town and Herman picked up speed, she lost her balance and fell. Herman was so excited to be speeding through the countryside that he didn't notice that Naomi had fallen off the back of the motorbike. After waiting hopefully for a while for him to come back, Naomi made her way back into town by hitching a lift.

It took Herman almost half an hour to realise that Naomi was no longer aboard. Shocked, he spent the rest of the day searching for her in the local hospitals. It was with great relief that he finally found her back at home and he promised to look after his little sister's best friend more carefully in future.

Naomi continued her friendship with Moishe and his sisters Shoshi and Rivka. Visiting Shoshi and her husband Mikki in Holon, Naomi would often babysit their young son, Yossi. This close friendship with Shoshi and Mikki was to prove an enduring one. She exchanged letters and the occasional visit with her dear friend Chaya, who had married a young man named Yisrael and was now living on Kibbutz Hamapil in the heart of the country. She continued to see Batsheva, her commanding officer in the army; Dov Levine, the soldier who had kept her company when she was in hospital on

Mount Scopus and Herman, who continued to look out for her. She was never without friends.

But she was closest of all to Sari and Pishta, whom she fondly referred to as Sarineni and Pishtabatchi, Aunt Sari and Uncle Pishta. Chana was always very busy working, as well as being involved in several Communist groups, so Naomi would often visit Sarineni on her own. On the eve of Rosh Hashanah – the Jewish New Year – 1950, Naomi arrived at Sari's and Pishta's house with a gramophone and some classical records, the first of many such evenings. They became like parents to her, telling her how to dress and advising her about life in general. She would often confide in them about Zvi and her fear that he was unfaithful and that the marriage would not work.

By the beginning of 1951, it was clear that Zvi was not going to return to Israel. He continued to write to Naomi and asked her to return to join him in Milan, where he had found a job. She didn't know what to do; she didn't want to leave Israel but she wanted to see Zvi and settle her marriage once and for all. She discussed at length with Sari and Pishta what would be the best course of action and they encouraged her to go to Milan to make up her mind, once and for all. They also advised their own daughter Chana to go to the US to study, as with so many war widows like Chana in Israel, Sari felt that Chana's options were severely limited. Both Chana and Naomi agreed that the advice given to them by Pishta and Sari was wise. But Chana was not yet ready to leave Israel and remained there for another year. In July 1951, sadly, Naomi left Israel, where she had been happy, so that she could face these crucial decisions.

As Naomi boarded a boat at Haifa, bound for Genoa, a young man offered her help with her suitcase. That night at dinner, she was bemused to find the waiter directing people away from her table until this same young man came to sit next to her. Years later, she would discover that this determined young man had tipped the waiter to ensure that nobody other than he would be allowed to sit with Naomi.

Asher Blake was a refugee from Berlin, having escaped to London from Germany in 1939. He and Naomi spent most of the evening chatting, sharing opinions about books and music and in general finding that they had a great deal in common. They had both been members of Hashomer Hatzair and had similar principles regarding Zionism. Both were refugees finding their way in a new country. In Berlin, Asher had been very involved in Hashomer and, under the guise of a teacher, he educated young Jews about the Facist regime and prepared them to escape Germany for life in Palestine. As a Jew in 1930s in Berlin he had suffered similar discrimination to Naomi. His strong will saw him involved in several fights on the streets with Fascists and his belief in Socialism almost led him to travel to Spain and fight in the Spanish Civil War. However, he understood the peril that his family were facing and focused his efforts on obtaining exit permits to enable his parents and sister to escape Germany in 1938 and make their way to Palestine.

As he was no longer a minor, he was unable to travel with them, so he remained in Germany until 1939, when family members arranged an invitation for him to enter the UK and he managed to smuggle himself out and reach London. Here he continued to be actively involved in Hashomer Hatzair and he remained in London throughout the war.

Over the next few days on the boat, Naomi played a lot of chess and usually won. She beat Asher but he seemed to be the only one of her male victims not to mind being beaten by a woman. And so they continued to share their stories. He was separated from his wife, Judith and five-year-old daughter, Helen, who had left England to go and live in Israel. Asher had joined them in Israel the previous year to try to rebuild his marriage but it had not worked out, so he was returning to London, downhearted. He was distressed at having to say goodbye for a second time to his daughter but meeting Naomi lifted his spirits.

Naomi in turn confided in Asher about Zvi and that she, too, was trying to make her marriage succeed. When the boat docked in Genoa, Naomi and Asher promised to keep in touch with each other and, while she nervously made her way to Milan, Asher continued to London.

In Milan, Naomi stayed with Zvi in a rented room of a small private house. Once she was reunited with him, she was full of hope. She found work as a Hebrew teacher in a small school where Zvi was also working part-time while training for the opera. However, it soon became evident that, during their time apart, Zvi had developed a relationship with another woman. After a couple of months, Naomi felt that she could no longer remain with him while he continued to seem so interested in other women, and she wrote to Sarineni and Pishtabatchi to tell them her feelings. She also wrote to Malchi and Shimi, who immediately sent her money so that she could come back to Tangier.

Naomi accepted their invitation and once more settled in with her sister and brother-in-law and their girls. She kept putting off the day when she would have to face Zvi and ask for a divorce but eventually she summoned up the courage to write to him and told him of her decision and her intention to return to Milan to carry it out. Zvi was extremely surprised by Naomi's boldness and at first tried to resist by refusing to give her a *get* (a Jewish religious bill of divorce), without which she would not be able to remarry in a synagogue.

This made Naomi even more determined and she went to speak to the headmaster and rabbi of the school where Zvi was still working, both of whom promised to try to persuade Zvi to comply. Her request was also backed up by a letter from Pishtabatchi in Israel. Eventually, Zvi relented and agreed to a divorce.

Even though Naomi knew that this was the right course of action, she nevertheless cried pitifully at this outcome. She had overcome one hurdle but now she had others to face. With no job and no place to live in Israel, she returned to Tangier and the welcoming home of Malchi and Shimi.

28

Gradually, she found she could express her past experiences and emotions through her sculpture

On Naomi's arrival in Tangier, she found a letter waiting for her. It was from Asher. She hadn't heard from him since they parted in Genoa and was very happy to do so now. They began to correspond. After much procrastination and discussion with Shimi and Malchi, Naomi agreed to meet Asher in Florence – eight months after their first meeting.

Once again, their shared views and interests – and the common experience of a failed first marriage – seem to draw them together. Moreover, being in Asher's presence made Naomi understand how unsuitable her marriage to Zvi had been. But her greatest wish was to return to Israel and so she was wary of making a commitment. Asher invited her to join him in England and, knowing how she felt about Israel, promised to do his utmost to find a job there so that they could return together.

Excited but unsure, Naomi wrote to Pishtabatchi and Sarineni seeking their advice and told Malchi and Shimi that she was seriously thinking of moving to London. She had anyway begun to feel herself to be a burden on her sister and brother-in-law in Tangier. And, having given up her house and her job, she had nowhere to return to in Israel. In these circumstances, life with a stable and serious man with a similar background to hers was very appealing. So it was that, in June 1952, with money sent to her by Asher, together with a bit extra from Shimi, Naomi set off for London.

London in the 1950s was still in the process of rebuilding after the war. Life was not easy for new immigrants. Asher, at that time, had a job as a carpenter for Ferry Aviation and worked very long hours. Naomi, on the other hand, couldn't speak English and was unable to find work. She enrolled in a language school to learn English and there befriended other new immigrants. Asher's friends also received Naomi warmly and she soon came to feel at home in London.

For all the hours that Asher worked, they were still struggling and when Naomi saw an advertisement in the *Jewish Chronicle* newspaper for a job with the Jewish National Fund as an events organiser, with prospects for promotion, she encouraged Asher to apply. He got the job – and with this new injection of money, they were able, two months after her arrival, to move from their room in Willesden to a one-bedroom flat in Temple Fortune, near Golders Green, in North West London.

Asher's new job in the JNF gave Naomi hope that he would soon be able to transfer his skills to Israel and perhaps work for the organisation in Jerusalem. So she was very excited when, in the spring of 1953, the JNF sent Asher to Israel on a working trip. Naturally, she accompanied him. They stayed with his sister in Haifa and then with Etu in Jerusalem. Naomi met Asher's mother and father and Asher met Sarineni and Pishtabatchi and both were accepted into each other's family.

Naomi was fervently hoping that, while in Israel, Asher would find some suitable job opportunities, but times were still very hard in Israel, with unemployment high. She returned to London disappointed but still nursed the hope that Asher's job would eventually enable them to move to Israel. However, after three months, Naomi's entry visa was due to expire. The only way for her to stay with Asher in London was to get married. She managed to overcome her fear of commitment – and on October 17, 1953, she and Asher were married in Willesden Green Synagogue. Poor but happy, they next went to Tangier so that Asher could at last meet Malchi and Shimi.

Back in London, Asher's work with the JNF organising events kept him busy several evenings a week. Naomi signed up for art classes to pass the time, while continuing to study English. She also found work as a Hebrew teacher. She enjoyed her art classes immensely and found herself quite adept at both pottery and sculpture, remembering the wooden dog that she had carved in Hadassah Hospital on Mount Scopus.

Despite the warm welcome of Asher's friends and her own friendships with other new immigrants, Naomi found the British rather cold – particularly the British Jews. Living in a predominantly Jewish area such as Temple Fortune, Naomi was disappointed to find that when she asked a neighbour for an egg she was directed to the nearest shop. Some people were friendly but many seemed to look down on foreigners and certainly did not know how to react to survivors.

Later, when they moved to Muswell Hill in North London, many of their non-Jewish neighbours introduced themselves and offered to help. On one occasion, however, when the next door neighbour was chatting over the fence – and telling Naomi: "if you need something, please don't hesitate to ask"

– she offered to show Naomi some of the local shops, "because some are owned by Jews and you have to be more careful". When Naomi told her she was Jewish, the neighbour's face turned bright red. She never said another word to Naomi, probably out of sheer embarrassment.

In particular, Naomi found, conversations about the Holocaust were taboo, which was difficult because she still felt the need to talk about it. Again, it was the British Jews who seemed particularly indifferent. Naomi supposed that they probably felt uncomfortable because they had not suffered. But she still found it hard to appreciate their reluctance to enter into any meaningful discussion. As a result, most of their friends were non-Jews or immigrants like themselves.

By the end of 1953, Naomi was pregnant and in July 1954 her son Jonathan was born. By this time, she and Asher had managed to obtain a loan and buy a house in Muswell Hill. With a child came new friendships with local mothers and she began to feel more settled. Nevertheless, her constant longing to return to Israel did not diminish and frequently caused friction between Asher and herself. Disappointed that Asher wasn't making it a priority to search for work in Israel – and sometimes out of sheer frustration with the English weather and the distant nature of the people – she would write to her friends in despair, declaring that, if the situation did not change, she would leave Asher and come back to Israel.

However, in 1959, when Jonathan was five and a second child, Anita, was born, Naomi was much more entrenched in the British capital, especially among her fellow young mothers. No longer able to attend regular evening art classes, she was now experimenting with clay at home in a corner of the kitchen. Beginning with pottery, over the years she moved on to clay sculpture.

Since Asher's job required him to travel to Israel from time to time and Naomi was able to accompany him, she was able to keep in touch with her friends. She and Asher strengthened the relationship with Shoshi – the eldest sister of Naomi's childhood friend Moishe – and her husband Mikki who had settled in Tel Aviv. They stayed in each other's homes as often as they could.

In later years, when Asher and Naomi travelled to Israel every year, Mikki and Shoshi would always meet them at the airport and, whatever the hour, their first stop would be Shuk Bezalel for felafel. In Haifa, Asher's parents and sister would always welcome them and, in Jerusalem, Sarineni and Etu would also have open doors.

Every visit involved a connection with their past – with Chaya at Kibbutz Hammapil; Rachel, Chaya's sister at Kibbutz Yakum and Asher's childhood friends from Hashomer Hatzair, Reuven Zif in Kibbutz Mishmar Haemek and Shimon Peles in Kibbutz Dalia. Finally in the early 1960s, when Chana returned with her husband Nissan to Israel, Naomi was able to resume this extraordinary friendship as well. Although these regular visits never quite satisfied her wish to return to Israel, they were a great joy.

As for Naomi's sisters and brothers, despite the great distance between them, they wrote to each and visited whenever the opportunity arose, with happy reunions for numerous barmitzvahs and weddings as their ten children grew older. In 1967, they all attended Jonathan's barmitzvah celebration in London. Moishe and his wife Rosa, from Caracas, Malchi and Shimi from New York, Ruchtu from Philadelphia and Sari all the way from Australia. They rarely missed an opportunity to reunite and the nature of their reunions were distinguished by constant laughter and Yiddish joke-telling.

After ten years with the JNF, Asher had developed excellent contacts in the Jewish and Israeli worlds and eventually found himself working with the Recanati Brothers, part of a successful banking family. His later work representing the Israel Discount Bank in London introduced them to many new friends in London, Tel Aviv and Jerusalem and although they never moved to Israel they spent a month every year there, visiting these new friends, as well as their childhood companions.

With Asher earning a good salary, Naomi could afford to be a full-time mother as well as develop her talent as a sculptor. In 1963, the family moved to a new home, where Naomi converted the garage into a studio – and the kitchen became clay-free. From this point, with a dedicated space for her work, and her children in school, she was able to concentrate on her sculpture and develop her talent away from figurative clay sculpture to abstract and semi-abstract forms, working in clay and polystyrene and casting in bronze and bronze resin.

Gradually, she found she could express her experiences and emotions of the past, which were so difficult to share with her London friends, through her sculpture. And she enjoyed considerable success. Over the years, Naomi Blake became recognised for her talent as a sculptor, with numerous exhibitions and commissions throughout the UK and in Israel.

The youngest of the ten Düm children, Naomi has survived Fishel, Ruchtu, Sari, Moishe and Malchi and fondly remembers their love of laughter. She has lived alone since 2003, when she lost her beloved Asher but she is constantly surrounded by her family of two children, one step-daughter, five grandchildren, six step-grandchildren and eleven step-great grandchildren.

Today, Naomi is proud of her achievements. Through her sculpture, she can honour the memory of her lost sisters, brothers and young cousins and, through her family, demonstrate her will to survive against the odds and her hope for the future.

POSTSCRIPT

POSTCRIPT

My mother the sculptor

I have so many childhood memories of my mother. Her loving, warm and generous nature, which I enjoy to this day; her stories about her life, which inspire me; her lullabies in numerous languages, which I loved; and sitting quietly for her when I was three years old so that she could do my sculpture portrait... which I hated.

All these memories became an important part of our family life. I remember watching her working on sculptures in our kitchen and then later in her studio, jealous of the attention she paid to her work but always feeling proud when she completed something.

Since those early days of ceramics and portrait sculpture, her work has developed in numerous ways. She moved quite quickly from the figurative portrait sculptures to more abstract pieces, from working in clay to working in polystyrene (she always said that she enjoyed giving life to such a lifeless material as polystyrene). These large, abstract sculptures often seemed to enclose and protect a form inside. At the same time, my mother found considerable meaning in her commissions in memory of the victims of the Holocaust.

Her involvement with the Council for Christians and Jews, for whom her first memorial sculpture was unveiled in 1973, marked her determination to promote understanding between faiths. Commissions on this theme followed from many synagogues, places of Jewish learning, and then from churches and cathedrals. Her work can now be seen throughout the UK, at Kingsbury Synagogue, Leo Baeck College, Yarnton Manor, Bristol Cathedral, St Botolph's Church and many other places.

In the late 1970s and early '80s, my mother's crouching and protected figures changed into a series of figures holding on to a sail, as if they were bracing themselves against a storm, for a series named *Man Against the Odds*.

Two of these pieces were subsequently placed in Israel, at the Tel Aviv University and in Ashkelon. These were followed by more open figures depicting bird forms in flight. I understood at that point that she was freeing herself from her past – something she confirmed in an interview with the *Guardian* in 1981.

What followed in the '80s and '90s were sculptures that focused on the human form, often unprotected but strong, underlining her faith in humanity. She continued to enjoy considerable success with commissions at Norwich Cathedral and Beth Shalom Holocaust Education Centre – and with private work that displayed a feminine, soft and flowing (maternal) style.

In the 1990s, Naomi met Jill and John Hutchins, owners of the Curwen and New Academy Gallery, and she has since held four successful solo exhibitions in their central London gallery. Her newest exhibition, in April 2014, *Naomi Blake: A Retrospective,* a book about her work, *Naomi Blake: Dedication in Sculpture* and a new website, www.naomiblake co.uk, show the development and volume of her work during her 60 years as a sculptor and detail more than 60 exhibitions and 70 sculptures unveiled in public places in the UK and Israel.

My mother's story was always with me, through her sculpture and through her openness about her life. While she expressed it through her sculpture, she always hoped that I would express it in words – and therefore talked about it openly when my brother and I were very young.

When I was nine years old, on holiday alone with her in Bournemouth, she decided to tell me her story in detail. I already knew that she had lost many family members and I knew that she had been in a concentration camp but now, she decided, was the time to tell me in full.

Every morning, we would order breakfast in bed and, over toast and baked beans, she told me about her life right from the beginning. It seems strange to say this but I enjoyed every moment. After finishing breakfast, I would snuggle up to her and she would talk. She spoke about Mukačevo, her family, the discrimination and hardship that followed, her journey to Auschwitz and her liberation. I shuddered at some revelations but laughed at others – for example, when she told me how she and her sister did not recognise each other with shaven heads at Auschwitz. I felt anger at the way she and her fellow prisoners were treated and sadness at the loss of the family I never met. I felt inspired by her journey to Palestine, great satisfaction that she found a new home, and pride that she showed so much courage as a solider.

You may think that a nine-year-old would be frightened and traumatised by this but somehow my mother was able to relate her experiences with the utmost calm, warmth and optimism, so that I always wanted to hear more. I was proud of her inner strength, her will to survive and her positive nature. Many talk of the children of survivors being adversely affected by their parents' experiences of the Holocaust but, for me, it was the opposite. My aunts and uncles were always full of love and laughter; my mother and her friends in Israel – Chaya, Chana, Sarineni, Etu and Shoshi – were all so welcoming and full of life that, although sadness was always a part of them, they never openly showed any signs of trauma. Quite the opposite: they were all progressive, open-minded and possessed of a strength of character that I remain in awe of to this day.

The titles of her most recent sculptures, *Glimmer of Hope* and *Towards Tomorrow*, which appear on the front covers of this book and the book about her sculpture and inspire this title, are expressions of this positive spirit.

As Naomi told the Guardian in 1981: "there's something positive in the human figure – there's a lot of good in people... With my past, if I were pessimistic, somehow, it wouldn't have been worthwhile surviving."

Today, despite the difficulties of old age, she retains her sense of humour, warmth and optimism. Over the past 20 years, she has confronted the death of close friends Sarineni, Etu and Shoshi, and her older brothers and sisters, Fishel, Ruchtu, Sari, Moishe and, most recently, her dearest Malchi. In 2003, she lost her greatest supporter when my father passed away. However, she continues to enjoy life with her friends in London and she remains in close contact with Chana and Chaya in Israel.

My brother Jonathan and I continue to take great pride in her achievements and in the Jewish heritage for which she fought so hard. Her five grandchildren, too, know that they are privileged to have such an accomplished and inspiring grandmother in their lives.

Anita Peleg, London, April 2014

Further information about Naomi Blake
can be found in the following sources:

Naomi Blake: Dedication in Sculpture
by Anita Peleg (2014)

www.naomiblake.co.uk

www.curwengallery.co.uk